from
Lee Hill
Christmas - 1968

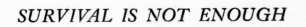

SURVIVAL IS NOT ENOUGH

BY D. W. CHARLTON

By These Things Men Live

Survival Is Not Enough

Survival
Is Not Enough

Messages for Our Times by

David W. Charlton

Exposition Press · New York

EXPOSITION PRESS INC., 386 Park Avenue South, New York 10016

FIRST EDITION

EP 44055

CONTENTS

SURVIVAL IS NOT ENOUGH

1   *IN THE BEGINNING*

A popular magazine carried an article on "Why I Left the Ministry." Many of us in the ministry have had our heartaches and our unhappy experiences. But there have been deep satisfactions and thrills, too, and a conviction of the message and mission of the church.

For one thing, I have continued in the ministry because of our "call" and our personal concern for people. As the pastor in a rural parish I once visited in the home of a shut-in. Though he was cut off from normal activities, his life bristled with interest. Sitting up in bed, he read newspapers, magazines, books. His hobby was medicine and he loved to discuss the make-up of the body—the billions of nerves in the brain and spinal column, the millions of sweat glands, the thousands of hairs on the head. But we also talked about the church and the community, and invoked some benediction on the household.

One woman who insisted on my regular calls could never remember my last name. "Call me by my first name, David," I suggested to her. That seemed to solve her problem.

A minister soon learns to pay close attention to names. Some members are hurt when the pastor fails to call them by name after spending some time on the charge. Others seem surprised and appreciative to hear their names. A memory for names is a valuable gift to the preacher.

One elderly man asked me to sing for him one of the old hymns of the church, but since I couldn't raise the tune, I quoted from the scriptures, which seemed to bring help and healing to his soul. A good woman, with a glow in her face, was cheered by the words: "And the peace of God, which passes all understanding, will keep your hearts and your minds in Christ Jesus" (Phil. 4:7).

An eighty-year-old man, long a caretaker for the church, passed away some years ago and I was asked to share the funeral service with the pastor. Before I left the church as minister I recognized his faithfulness to the church, his unbroken record of attendance every Sunday for many years. So long had he opened the doors of the church, placed the hymn books, rung the bell, that he seemed to be a part of the old place. At the funeral service the family was reminded of the words that seemed so fitting for him: "Well done, good and faithful servant" (Matt. 25:23).

I have sought an unfailing love for people and tried to deserve the respect that many show a minister. But I claim no such recognition as shown by one little girl who approached her pastor on the porch, then ran to the kitchen and exclaimed, "Oh, mother, come quickly! God is at the door." Surely that experience would make anyone feel very humble.

Now, unless guarded, pastoral visits become too long and indulge in light chatter. My little granddaughter occasionally accompanied her father, who closed some of his calls with a prayer. One day during a talkfest around the table at our family reunion, she grew tired and fell on her knees, saying, "Let us pray."

As Oliver Goldsmith said of the Parson, in tribute to his father:

> But in his duty prompt at every call,
> He watch'd and wept, he pray'd and felt for all: . . .
> Beside the bed where parting life was laid,
> And sorrow, guilt, and pain, by turns dismay'd.

Moving on, preaching has been given emphasis in my ministry, and I have tried to offer my best in the pulpit. Even so, an old sea captain remarked one day, "That first sermon was the poorest I ever heard you preach. Why did you preach that sermon on your first Sunday?" As the weeks unfolded, however, there were some encouraging words.

Morning hours were reserved for study, and it was my desire to grow a bit each year.

In another parish a little girl told me that she discussed the sermons with her mother at the dinner table. She remembered some of the stories, it appeared, and caught some of the ideas they were intended to illustrate.

Hearing me speak about the Trinity—Father, Son, and Holy Spirit—at one of the services, she asked, "Do you mean we have three gods?" I was surprised and somewhat baffled by the question from so young a person.

Speaking in child language, I told of the boy who had an uncle across the seas. He had never seen him, but he received letters from this relative, and was remembered with presents at Christmas. The uncle was a real father to the youth, who was grateful for his tenderness and love. One day the uncle sent his son to America, and the son came to see the boy and told him about his "father" back home in England.

Thus the child learned something of the Father-God, who gives good things to his children, and of the Son who tells us about the Father, even Christ. Then Christ reminded us, "I will pray the Father, and he shall give you another Comforter, that he may abide with you forever" (John 14:16). "He shall testify of me," Christ said. He meant that God's presence, understanding, and power would abide in our hearts. That is the work and activity of the Holy Spirit.

Moreover, I have felt there is some value in the proper use of humor, even in the pulpit. As John Wesley said, "Sour godliness is the devil's religion."

A chuckle could lift a load from a heavy heart. A young man lost both legs in a serious accident and someone expressed regret for the tragedy. "Oh, it isn't so bad," said the victim. "In fact it solved a problem for me. They were always cold anyway."

Some of our differences could be solved in a gracious compromise. Lincoln and his wife had some disagreement about the color of paint for their home. His wife insisted on yellow. He wanted green. "What did you do?" asked a friend. "We compromised," Lincoln replied, "and painted it yellow."

I believe in the living Presence and experience in religion.

A pastor reminded me of the little boy who was afraid to go to sleep in the dark. His mother tried to cheer him up by telling the youth that God was present in the darkness as well as the daytime. The boy gathered up his courage one night and walked down the hall to his room. The mother followed out of sight. Soon after the young fellow entered the room, she heard him say, "God, if you are here, don't move an inch or you'll scare me to death." To the spiritually mature person, God is a very present help in the time of trouble and along the journey of life.

Too much religion has lost the note of joy and good cheer, spiritual radiance.

To give balance to preaching, I followed the church calendar, and gave emphasis to special days like Easter and Christmas. I was aware, too, that the church must have a word from God on the alcohol problem, race relations, and world peace.

Underlying these meditations is the conviction that God is still in charge of the universe, and that we can find wisdom and guidance in a time of change and uncertainty. I have also felt the need of the daily disciplines of study, devotional readings, and prayer.

I hold that while man has achieved control of much of his outward surroundings, he lacks control of himself. To encompass spiritual mastery our lives must be God-centered and committed to Christ. Though the earth has shrunk in dimension, the dimension of our minds and souls must be widened for the survival of civilization.

We may well ponder the words that Jesus read in the synagogue: "The spirit of the Lord is upon me, because the Lord has anointed me to bring good tidings to the afflicted, he has sent me to bind up the broken hearted, to proclaim liberty to the captives, and the opening of the prison to those who are bound. . . ." (Isa. 61:1).

READ: Genesis 1:27–31; John 1:1–8,23
PRAYER: We thank thee, O Lord, for the high calling of God in Christ Jesus. In all our work, begun, continued, and ended in Thee, may we glorify Thy holy name. Amen.

2 TIME ON OUR HANDS

As we hang a new calendar on the wall we are aware of the passing of time. But to young people time drags its feet. Birthdays and other anniversaries are slow to come. Exciting events are anticipated.

Older people are inclined to look backward. In a play by James Barrie, a passenger hails a bus and shouts to the driver, "Go back ten years!"

We face the importance and pressure of time. The Greek language has two words for time: *chronos* and *kairos*. The first denotes duration of time, measured by clock or calendar. *Kairos* defines time as God-given possibility or opportunity.

Conscious of the clock and under pressure, a man said that he had been unable to read a small book in the course of weeks. "It's awful," he exclaimed; "we squeeze in so little of reading." Some say they do not have time for church. They do not use time in the larger sense of *kairos*.

Someone made an estimate of how the average person seventy years of age disposed of his time: "He spent six years in eating, eleven working, eight amusing himself, twenty-four sleeping, five and a half washing and dressing, three talking, and six months in church."

One man told of spending an hour and a half a day reading the newspapers. That was out of balance, he felt. He rearranged his schedule, and spent more time with magazines and books.

An American traveling in the Far East had two watches, one for local time and another for the time back home. . . . More important, do we employ our time as *kairos*, opportunities for self-improvement and self-giving—God's time?

We think of time in the sense of past, present, and future.

Some have spoken of "the dead past"; but is the past really dead? The fact is, we are in a continuous stream of life. Children have come out of homes that were a godsend or a drag on them. They will reflect in large measure the kind of surroundings and training they have received.

The alcoholic, for instance, is a product of his past, of influences within and without. The character of any person, in truth, is determined by the factors that have played upon his life.

The saints also reflect the past influences. Someone spoke of an old minister whose coming was like turning on the light and whose presence was a benediction. His life was wrought out of his past activities—study, meditation, witnessing for God.

We live only in the present. The cowboy philosopher Will Rogers was asked: "If you had only forty-eight hours to live, how would you live them?" He replied, "One at a time."

While God says today, man says tomorrow. Many have good intentions, but are inclined to wait for another day to do anything about them. As the legend goes, the demons were once discussing the obstacles they could put in the path of men on earth. One suggested, "Tell men there is no God." Another chimed in, "Say to them the Bible is a myth." A third replied, "Just tell them there is no need for promptness; wait until tomorrow." So procrastination is both the thief of time and the pitfall of many people.

A favorite word with John Wesley was *now*. He was ever achieving something today and pursuing the goal of the Kingdom of God. Another vigorous Christian leader was David Livingstone. His motto was, "Fear God and work hard." The living present is of supreme importance.

We must also face the future. While foresight and wise planning are urged, they are not, however, the same as possessing the future. The late W. E. Sangster reminded us of men whose vast dreams and designs were unfulfilled. The renowned Cecil Rhodes planned big things for himself and Africa, but he died at forty-nine moaning, "So much to do; so little done."

A pastor received a tearful letter from a young girl informing him of the death of her father. "He was full of plans for the future," she wrote. "But he suddenly collapsed and died."

Some have glowing expectations for the future. A business-man said he wanted to catch up on his reading and write books when he retired. But when that time came around he had lost all desire to achieve his ambition. The mood and motive were lost; the spell was gone.

Nor should we forget that we must trust the future. "Though the heavens fall, we must keep faith," said Henry Hitt Crane. "Believe in yourself. Believe in the essential integrity of the universe. Believe in your God."

Facing the unknown, we find confidence and courage to meet the present, with the assurance that our lives are in God's hands. As the intrepid explorer to the South Pole, Edward Wilson, faced the rigors of bitter cold and blizzards and the frightful difficulties of transportation, he exclaimed, "So I live, knowing I am in God's hands, whether I live a long time, full of good works, or die tomorrow."

In the process of maturing, we may go on from the dream to the deed, from insight to action, from conviction to life. Unless the deed is done, the creed comes to naught; unless the building rises, the blueprint is wasted.

Times comes alive when we are alert to present opportunities, and face the future with faith and high resolve.

READ: Psalm 90

PRAYER: Make us thankful, O Lord, for the past; alert to the present; trustful and hopeful for the future. Amen.

THE RULES OF THE ROAD

A son, Willie Keith, receives a letter from his ailing father in *The Caine Mutiny* by Herman Wouk. As the parent approaches the end of his journey, he has pangs of remorse over his failure to give guidance and help to his son along the way.

"I will mail you a Bible before I go to the hospital," he writes. "Get familiar with the words. You will never regret it. Think of me when you come to the crossroads. For my sake, for the sake of the father who took the wrong turns, take the right ones."

So many people take the wrong roads. "They waste their years," as Charles M. Crowe pointed out. It's easy to lose the way.

Some are lost in the fog of fear and anxiety. Counseling with a woman in the hospital some time ago, I found she was overanxious about her children. When she realized her fears had no basis in fact, she let go of her burden and was soon on the road to health.

Others are wandering around in the cloud of alcoholism. Some five and a half million people in this country are alcoholics, with possibly an equal number on the verge of becoming so. These people are in trouble with their addiction, and many are on the broad way of heartbreak and sorrow.

Still others are like the prodigal son who strayed away in the weakness of the flesh. There are those, too, who are like the elder son, resentful of his brother.

Look now for direction in our journey. There are signposts for guidance and other help along the way.

A tourist asked a bystander for directions to a certain town. "If you continue in the direction you are going, it's about twenty-five thousand miles," he said. "But if you turn around, it's about five miles." We can waste the years by going far out of the way.

There are directions along the straight way for those who seek it. Someone told of the woman who was hiking in unfamiliar territory. The ranger gave her a compass and showed her how to use it. Tramping far into the woods, however, she got lost and wandered in circles. When she finally thought of the compass and glanced at it, she regained her sense of direction and was able to complete her hike. There is an inner compass to enable us to travel the disciplined way of a Christian.

Look also at the signpost, "Curve, Slow Down." Life, even like many twisting roads, doesn't always move in a straight course, with no upsets or uncertainties.

One woman traveled cautiously, fearfully at times, over the Great Smoky Mountains, turning many sharp curves and hanging over wide spaces. Fortunately she overtook a truck with a friendly driver who had the same destination in view, and who offered to lead the way for her. There's leading and help along the way for those who look above and beyond themselves, and are not too self-reliant.

There are unknown experiences beyond the bend of the road. Who has not faced setbacks and disappointments? A patient looked ahead to a serious operation. The way must have seemed very dark and uncertain for her. But she made her plans in trust and hopefulness.

One of the most arresting signs a tourist observes on a super-highway is: "Food and Fuel, —— Miles Ahead." These words may remind us, not only of a possible need to refuel the car, but a chance to rest and renew body and mind. Continued travel without a break could mean fatigue, drowsiness—less care and safety in driving.

I received a marine and his attractive wife into the church some years ago. During the summer vacation they were on their way to their home town in another state. To save time and expense, they traveled very late at night. The man fell asleep at the wheel, and the car went out of control. Result: wife and baby killed!

As the body needs replenishing, so the inner man needs renewal. In a fast-moving age, many do not stop for worship on Sunday. A father remarked to a pastor, "When summer comes my boy will not be at church; he will be on the water, fishing." For depth dimension in life, one must take time for spiritual disciplines of meditation and study.

Moving on, a "No U Turn" sign may appear at the intersection. Here we may check our destination. The traffic light may suggest a needed turnabout in the way. If we are headed wrong, about-face or repentance could mean a vast difference— either faith and fulfillment, or frustration. Paul's swap of sides on the Damascus road changed the course of history.

In his momentous decision, the apostle found the Way in Christ, and from that time forth he pressed on toward the goal. The purpose, "This one thing I do," made the journey an adventure and dedication for him.

E. B. White wrote in one of his essays of a trip to his home in Maine. He referred to the late editor of *Harper's*, Berhard De Voto, who once traveled the same highway and lamented that the whole route had been ruined by commercialism at its worst.

But White caught the haunting atmosphere and beauty of the homeward journey. These men viewed the highway differently, perhaps because of the different goals they had in mind. De Voto was going to an uninspired speaking engagement, White was on his way home.

So, in terms of the Christian life, the final goal sheds its dim or glowing light on the Way.

READ: Matthew 7:13–14; Hebrews 12:1–2

PRAYER: Be our guide, O Lord, our stay and strength on the journey of life. May we endure as seeing Him who is invisible, even to the end. In Christ's name. Amen.

A two-year-old boy surprised his father by using a word he had heard from other children, "Martians," meaning inhabitants of Mars. Another word used in this complex time is "payola," meaning bribe or illegal payoff.

Look magazine published an article some time ago on "The Age of Payola." It disclosed, on the basis of a survey, that less than ten per cent of the people interviewed felt that honesty was a prime requisite for success. Most Americans seemed to condone the rigged television show when it involved a chunk of money. Cheating was accepted as part of the normal pattern of conduct. Anything goes when it meets with popular approval.

Consider the moral state of the nation. A letter came to me some time ago which reflected the moral muddle of our time. It urged: do something about obscene literature, shocking movies, the problem of alcoholism. . . .

A Duke professor taught a Bible course in our church, in 1964. He spoke of the wild parties staged by the young men and women of our colleges. "If you see what I do," said the teacher, "there is a breakdown in our moral and spiritual life."

The crime bill for the country soared to twenty billion dollars, according to Bishop Eugene M. Frank. "Illegitimacy has increased three hundred per cent in ten years," he stated. "Pornography has become a five-hundred-million-dollar-a-year business."

Meanwhile suicides have leaped to twenty-five thousand annually, with many unsuccessful attempts and others who have been on the rugged edge of self-destruction.

Fallout of the spirit is evident, too, in the moral emptiness

and meaninglessness of our time. Norman Vincent Peale told of
a call to a fashionable home in New York. Seeing the palatial
place, he wondered for a moment, "What could be lacking
here?"

As he mused on the scene, he ventured a word to the woman
who lived so elegantly: "Anyone who has the privilege of
living in a room like this must be both deeply grateful and very
happy."

Walking over to the mahogany desk, the woman opened it
and pulled out a pearl-handled revolver. "Dr. Peale," she went
on, "I would have used this on myself but for the embarrassment
it would have caused my friends and loved ones. I am utterly
miserable inside."

So material things alone do not make life full and happy.
Our relationship with God must be right for inner peace and
strength of character.

Consider some of the pressures of today that make people
act as they do. For one thing, people wield an influence over us.
"What they think of us," wrote Albert E. Day, "agitates us
more than what God thinks of us. We court their favor more
consistently than we seek to please God."

As a reporter expressed it, "You want to be a part of things,
don't you? You want to be accepted, to belong? You want to be
a regular, normal guy? You don't want to be odd, eccentric?
So keep step! Cooperate, compromise, conform, if you want to
get along with people."

Another trend toward conformity is that of speed and pre-
occupation with things. Rockets must attain a speed of twenty-
five thousand miles an hour, or seven miles a second, in order
to go into orbit. This mania for speed carries over into the business of living.

People are in a great hurry. Young people want to be adults
overnight. Older people are trying so hard to get ahead, they
miss the beauty and joy of living. It takes time to grow a human
life—mature, useful, Christlike.

There are efforts at thought-control. Ideas must fit into a
certain pattern, or a person is suspect. Extremists would pour

the thoughts of people into their mold; label them as dangerous or even drive them out of their jobs. Conform, conform, conform!

Paul was on solid ground when he said, "Don't let the world squeeze you into its mold, but let God remold your mind from within."

We are to aspire to live in conformity to the mind and spirit of Christ. To be cast in his mold is to have release from ourselves and to have a larger fulfillment.

The story goes that a young prince was kidnapped and taken to South America. Some twenty years later he learned of his royal heritage. Then the man affirmed, "I am a prince. I must live up to what I am." That belated knowledge and awareness changed his life. An impotent title is meaningless, but a meaningful title can transform our lives into the image of Christ.

A spiritually oriented person seeks to find the purpose and do the will of God.

When a group of children were asked to describe the most beautiful thing they had ever seen, they gave various answers. One spoke of the scenic view from the mountaintop. Another referred to the color and blazing beauty of the woods in autumn. A third youth told of the thrill he had in seeing the rising moon over the waters at night.

But one boy had a memorable image of Holman Hunt's portrait of Christ in the Garden of Gethsemane. "The most beautiful thing I have ever seen," he said, "is a picture of Jesus praying in the garden that he would do God's will." By doing his will we may conform to his image, and help to create a new social order for mankind.

In the words of Paul: "Don't let the world squeeze you into its mold, but let God remold your mind from within" (Rom. 12:1 [Phillips trans.]).

READ: Romans 12:1–21

PRAYER: Stir us up, O Lord; let us not be careless and complacent when the house of civilization is on fire. Amen.

Someone told of a farmer-landlord who ordered pecan trees and had them set out. Years afterwards when the owner of the farm checked on the trees, he found persimmons on them. Now the trees were reclassified, not by the labels but by the fruit. As the Bible says, "By their fruit you shall know them."

Fruit of the spirit is "love, joy, peace, patience, kindness, goodness . . . self-control" (Gal. 5:22 ff.). The quality of a Christian is to bear much fruit, to show forth the spirit of Christ.

A tree must have roots. Many people seem to feel they can be Christians without keeping in touch with Christ, the vital source of spiritual life. Observe the neglect of Bible reading and study, and of spiritual disciplines. "Have you read the scriptures?" Jesus repeatedly asked the disciples, and the Hebrew poet often meditated upon the Word (Ps. 1).

A young man who worked away from home received a package of cake from his mother every week. When he went home for his vacation he said to his parent, "Mother, you shouldn't do it. All this you are doing for me is too much." He also reminded her of her many chores at home. "Too much," his mother replied. "My son, think how much more I could do for you if you liver nearer." How much more Christ could do for us if we lived closer to him!

Good rootage for depth of character should begin in the home. The Hebrew people laid great store on religious training and the spiritual atmosphere of the home. Today too much time is devoted to all kinds of television programs, and little thought given to the growth of the inner life. A spattering of general knowledge comes, but wisdom lingers.

We are told of a group of teenagers who were on a dark

mission. One youth had the courage to turn back. When asked for an explanation of his break with the boys, he spoke of the Christian influences in his home, the spiritual roots that kept him steady and strong.

Moreover, the Bible speaks of a tree planted by the river of water. It was kept fresh and fruitful. A widely known surgeon, had a custom of wearing a fresh rose in the lapel of his coat. His friends wondered how the flower kept so fresh and fragrant. He explained that the stem of the rose rested in a small tube of water concealed in his coat.

Does our religion tend to fade? Does the Bible seem to be dry and meaningless? Are we losing interest in the church? We may need to revive and strengthen our faith, to give it vigor and freshness, by drinking of the water of life.

A new experience may enable us to discover a vital relationship with God. A woman was thrilled by the rare beauty of the sunset painted by an artist whose insight and skill captured its grandeur and glory. The woman remarked to the painter, "I have lived here all these years, but I never really saw the sunset until you came along."

We may have a new beginning with God as we confront Him in a new and revealing worship experience. A Salvation Army officer knelt at the spot where General William Booth was converted, and cried, "Do it again, Lord, do it again!" With such an inflow of the spirit, there may be a breakthrough, new insight and release of spiritual power.

When the tree is good it will bear a high quality of fruit. A woman once attended a Bible class and was moved by the spirit to begin a new life with Christ. "Do you remember what an untidy housekeeper I used to be before I studied the Bible?" she asked her husband. "Look at the house now," she went on. "I was known, too, to be the longest-tongued woman in the village and spent most of my time in spreading gossip and scandal. Now I go to help my neighbors."

So the fruit of the spirit makes life finer, cleaner, better, happier. It also makes us more considerate of each other, and establishes smoother and more brotherly relationships.

The Bible tells us that the tree should be pruned, dead limbs cut away. Bad tempers, ugly dispositions, lust of the flesh, the greedy and grasping nature, race prejudice, should be pruned away. Only then can we yield the fruit of the spirit, and be full worthy of the title "Christian."

In Japan comparatively little land can be cultivated, but all available land is made fertile and productive. With the explosion of population, waste and unproductiveness must be eliminated.

E. Stanley Jones, who has spent much time as a missionary in Japan, told of an apple that is twice the size of the ordinary fruit. He described a man who staggered through a station with one turnip across his back. He informed us of strawberries three inches in length.

Pressed for more land to feed their teeming millions, the Japanese have achieved amazing results in fertilizing and pruning. As Christians we are to do some pruning, and to be growing and fruit-bearing.

An older man stood in a meeting and told a group about his disagreeable disposition years ago. "But the Lord has led me on," he affirmed; "I feel I am more understanding, and have more love for people and more of the spirit of the Lord."

But the final test of the Christian religion in our world is the kind of people who claim faith in Him. What example are we setting before men? What is the impact of our lives on the world community? Wasn't it said of the early Christians that they outlived and outloved others, and "turned the world upside down"?

A cultured Brahman said, "I don't like the Christ of your creeds and the Christ of your churches." Then he spoke of his admiration for Christ's healing ministry and his humanitarian work, the spirit of the cross and self-giving. We must go much further as members in bearing the fruit of the spirit.

READ: Matthew 7:15–20; Galatians 5:16–25

PRAYER: Help us, O Lord, to be Christian in spirit and in truth, and to bear the fruit of the spirit—love, joy, kindness, self-control, and a life of service. Amen.

6   *WHEN PLANS ARE UPSET*

Two women, in gales of laughter and good spirits, were on their way to attend a celebration on a cold day. Stopping the car at a friendly old inn, they stepped out onto a treacherous glaze of ice. One of the ladies went down, with a leg twisted under her. "Broken," said the doctor on examination. "Your leg will be in a cast for two months."

"We were so happy," moaned the victim. "Isn't it always like that?"

Handicaps or interruptions are common in daily life. Foul weather blights our plans, criticism and misunderstanding hurt, loss of a job disappoints us, ill health sets us back.

The Gallup Poll inquired of a group about their reaction when they felt let down or cheated in life. "I go out to the pasture and try to forget the whole thing," one man groaned. "I go alone to dinner and to the movies," declared a wife. A husband turned on the TV.

"When life comes up the hard way, more commonly we swallow barbiturates and tranquilizers; we lash out at people we care about . . . we come down with various kinds of psychosomatic illnesses," wrote Artis Whitman.

"Yet there are some who grow faint and weary, and who meet every opportunity and challenge with a sniveling whisper: What's the use with my handicaps?" said C. William Fisher.

But what may seem a misfortune or handicaps could have a brighter side. The Chinese philosopher Lin Yutang told the story of a man whose only horse wandered away. His neighbors came to express regret for the misfortune. But a week later the beast came home, bringing with him a whole herd of wild horses. Another time the old man's son met with an accident and was crippled. He was therefore exempted from the draft, and the father rejoiced.

A sense of values affects our everyday lives. Our eyes may be glued on the tangible thing, unaware of the unseen, invisible world where "the tissues of destiny are woven."

So we may be upset and life may tumble in by the things that happen to us. "Consider that money may slip through our fingers, health fail under the weight of years, friends and loved ones disappear down the road from which no one returns. All things of the earth are transient as the wind," Everett W. Parmer reminded us.

A famous newspaper columnist, Victor Reisel, was blinded by a cruel twist of fate. A hoodlum splashed a glass of sulphuric acid into his eyes as a brutal protest against the reporter's uncovering of his crimes. Still active against the underworld, however, Reisel exclaimed, "If you can't help it, you can't spend your life in one constant moan against it. . . . But I am less dazzled by material things. I have a deeper hunger for the blazing light which the right (and truth) always need. Even in darkness, I can see that light."

Events of the moment need not upset a person whose eyes are on the lasting things of life. A country preacher served his churches lovingly for many years, and at sixty-three years of age expected an extension of time. But one day he received a letter from the officials of the charge that hit him like a bombshell. After some words of praise, it stated bluntly, "We feel that a younger man is needed." Despite the dismissal letter, he continued to love his people for a season and to finish his work in a kind and cheerful manner.

We are in need of spiritual resources to meet the varied experiences of life. Many lives tumble in because they lack the faith to declare with Paul, "I can do all things in him who strengthens me."

A newspaper carried the story of two young men who faced a shocking event in their lives, and the circumstances were very much alike. Jilted by his girl friend, one boy left a note of despair on the bridge. "I am going to jump off this bridge," he wrote. "Everybody is against me, and the only one I ever loved is mad at me. I think this is the only way out." Then he leaped.

The other young man, a corporal in the Air Force, was also jilted by his girl. But the sun broke through the overhanging clouds, and he wrote a song that became a popular hit. It yielded him some twenty thousand dollars. So often "the sweetest songs are those that tell of saddest thought."

I am reminded, too, of the farmer who hired a young man to help him with his work. When the farmer asked the fellow what he could do, he got the startling reply, "I can sleep when the wind blows." Though the farmer didn't understand the statement, he employed the prospect.

Somewhat later a heavy wind and rain came during the night. The farmer took his lantern and went out to check on the premises. He found everything in good shape. The barn doors and shutters were well closed and barred. The cows were bedded down in clean straw. The windmill had been shut off and secured. So the farmer knew what the employee meant when he said he could sleep well when the wind blew.

When the storms of life howl and beat upon us, we need not wring our hands in panic if we have serenity and peace, the inner resources of the spirit. As someone said, "We can prepare for the worst by living every day at our best."

READ: Philippians 4:8–13

PRAYER: Eternal God, give us the foresight to do the best we can and the insight to leave the rest with Thee. Amen.

7   A FAITH TO LIVE BY

Translators were unable to give the usual meaning of "faith" in a certain language or dialect. So they expressed the concept of faith in simple, understandable terms as that "inner power which gets you around the corner."

What we really believe in moves us to action. "Ideas," someone said, "are more powerful than bombs." Explosives would not be dropped from space if good will and common concern prevailed.

Faith gets us around the corner, carries us over the hump, because it means confidence in ourselves and in a higher Power. The gospel of confident living has a needed emphasis. We can never climb the heights by staying in the valley of doubts, misgivings, and fears. Many people triumph in life by believing a thing can be done, and doing the impossibles.

The famous football coach Knute Rockne told the men on his team, "I will not have a boy on my team with a inferiority complex. He must believe that he can accomplish things."

"Our belief in a doubtful undertaking," said William James, "is the one thing that assures the successful outcome of the venture." And Christ affirmed, "If thou canst believe, all things are possible."

Faith includes purpose and drive in life. People often move aimlessly, in circles, without goals or destination in view. Life is thus unmotivated, and energy is not confined or directed.

A pastor once told of a well-to-do man who came to his study and unfolded a story of futility and frustration, despite his success in business. "I would be willing to leave everything I possess with you," he told the pastor, "if I could find happiness." He had not discovered the real meaning of life, nor the joy of finding a challenging purpose in life, or an object of high devotion.

A man's purpose may change overnight, and instead of heartache, he may find a heap of good living. The noted pastor W. E. Sangster was asked to call on a young man who had a nervous breakdown. He found the young fellow in the doldrums. Life was dull, drab, with all pain and nothing of pleasure, he felt. "It isn't worth living," he moaned. Weeks passed, and the task of helping to heal the man seemed rather hopeless.

Then something happened. The young man fell in love with a girl. A new, bright day dawned for him. The birds sang their hearts out. Flowers were never more beautiful. How glorious to be alive!

When a man found Christ some years ago, he remarked that the fields, the cattle, everything, seemed different. Like Paul he found a new life in Christ and could declare, "For me to live is Christ."

Faith releases inner resources. A physician testified, "Prayer is a force as real as terrestial gravity. . . . I have seen men, after all other therapy had failed, lifted out of disease and melancholy by the serene effort of prayer."

A member of Alcoholics Anonymous told of his victory over the ravages of drink. He described his triumph in terms of a unique watch he was seeking. It would not only indicate the hours and minutes of the day, but would tell the days of the month and the phases of the moon. It seemed that such a watch would have everything but running water. If such a watch needed repairs, it could not be taken to an ordinary jeweler, he said, but would have to go back to its maker. So our complicated lives must be remolded by the redeemer of our souls.

By faith we are able to lay hold on divine resources, and renew our strength as we link our lives to infinite power. In times of testing and crisis we are upheld by the inner power of God.

In time of difficulty and distress it's a living faith that sustains us. But too often people look to the Lord only in the time of trouble and put little trust in Him in normal times. When the tide of battle went against the Union forces at the battle of Bull Run, a group of so-called atheists met for prayer. Curious, Lincoln went to the leader of the group and asked him to explain his action. "Well," said the unbeliever, "atheism seemed all right in the time of peace, but when the disaster of Bull Run befell us, we felt that something beyond our power had to be done."

So when our own sources of strength and endurance are exhausted, we reach for spiritual and divine resources. But our strength should be renewed daily lest it be chiseled away in our contact with the world and our overriding fears.

In our day-by-day confident trust in God we are delivered from debilitating and defeating fears. Fears of insecurity, illness, and death may create panic in the soul.

Counseling a woman some time ago, a pastor listened to her pathetic story of the uncertainties of health, her future home, financial insecurity. Despite her ownership of property, money in the bank, and regular income, fears were gnawing away at her life, leaving her in a mood of depression. Then the pastor reminded her of the words of the scripture: "Trust in the Lord with all your heart. . . . In all your ways acknowledge him . . ." (Prov. 3:5).

Consider the meaning of faith in the sickroom or in time of sorrow. We read of the frail little girl who was to have an operation without anesthesia. Giving her a coin, the surgeon told her to read the words she found on the piece of silver during the operation, and then he would ask her what she had read.

After the ordeal the physician said, "You have been a brave little girl. Now tell me what you read on the coin." She replied, "I read, In God we trust." Not only was she pleased with the money given her, but she would never forget the words that seemed to help her in the time of trouble.

The words of the scripture, too, have helped to heal many troubled hearts. Time and again the load has been lifted by the presence and the promises of God, by the assurances given by understanding and concerned pastors. The sorrowing have felt the touch of a God that cares and have been undergirded with His strength.

In this day of testing for individuals and nations we may be reminded of the ordeal of Moses in the wilderness. Having braved the armies of Pharaoh and the waters of the Red Sea, he led the children of Israel out into the desert country. Out in the wide stretches of wastelands, there was a dearth of water and food. In need of these necessities, the people cried out against their leader, "Why did Moses bring us out here to die? Would God we had died in the land of Egypt!"

With great faith and courage Moses said to his people, "Let us go forward." The way is not back to the fleshpots of Egypt, but onward to the new day of destiny. Crisis means both opportunity and challenge.

Some people begin in life with high hopes and enthusiasm, but when difficulties and disappointments come, they fall away. Resentments, failures, and blunders of bygone days should be laid aside. We will accomplish nothing by harking back to them. The way is forever forward. With faith we not only believe, but resolve under God to do something about our belief.

The church and every good institution in our land has been made possible by men of faith. Nor will the Cause be advanced by those who drag their feet or hold back, nor by the indifferent people who do not seem to care. We thank God for those who have slipped their hands into the hands of God, and said, "We are ready to go forward."

READ: Hebrews 11:32–12:2
PRAYER: Increase our faith, O God, as we seek to follow Thee. May we realize that by Thy help the impossible may be brought to pass. Amen.

Often happiness is thought of in terms of fortune's favor, luck, or gratified desire. Many are the well-wishers for the success of budding youth or newly married couples.

Do we not desire happiness above everything else? The word is included in the Declaration of Independence as one of our "unalienable rights."

The concept of happiness as disclosed in the Sermon on the Mount is that men should aspire to the best kind of life in relationship to God. The new dimension of life includes the spirit of love, trust, and the ideals voiced by the psalmists and prophets.

1. What happiness is not! It is not something to be sought directly, but a by-product of life. It is not to be found by the escape route of drink or mere pleasure-seeking.

A child was asked what he thought God was like. He replied, "God is the kind of person who is always snooping around to see if anyone is enjoying himself, so he can put a stop to it."

But Christ was no killjoy or "pale Galilean." He attended the wedding festival at Cana, brought health and healing to many, and delighted in the beauty of the open spaces.

Happiness is not what you *have* but what you *are*. Some parents with large families and few things in the home are very happy in their relationship with each other. Some have everything money can buy, yet are very unhappy.

Nor does happiness depend entirely on *where* we live. Young men were once visiting a small town. One of the group declared, "This is the deadest place we have ever seen." Still, the place was something of a paradise to the inhabitants of the town. Recall, too, that the Master spent his short life in a small, impoverished, hilly country.

2. What happiness *is*! It's a kind of life that has deep roots in religion. It comes from within rather than from without.

In the Bible the happy people are those who show the spirit of goodness, kindness, and love. They have understanding and good will toward their fellow men, and seek the ways of peace.

As we have seen, things alone do not bring happiness. This is true not only of Americans, but of mankind. We as a nation have everything in the way of money, education, beauty. Still, many of our people are restless, bored, ridden with neuroses.

Our sense of values is confused. The story is told of a youth who was rescued from drowning by a sailor at the risk of his life. Seeing the boy and his mother on the street somewhat later, the sailor naturally expected some word of appreciation. Instead, the mother asked in anger, "What did you do with the boy's cap?"

Some living solely for the present and the tangible cannot take the loss of money, and turn to self-destruction. Others who suffered reverses in their fortune have become embittered against the world.

But some set their affections on the intangibles of culture, beauty, art, and the lasting realities of the spirit. A noted author and clergyman, Jeremy Taylor, had his home plundered and confiscated because of his stand on certain social issues of his day. Out of the ashes of adversity he declared, "They have left me sun and moon, and a loving wife, and friends. I look upon the merry countenances of children, and I believe in God's care and providential leading." In his later years his writings were widely acclaimed. In giving priority to spiritual values he found the higher happiness.

So happiness is not dependent on outward circumstances, but is the condition of the heart, the fruit of the spirit.

3. A precondition for happiness is to have a sense of appreciation and gratitude. As one man remarked, "I have lived most of my life on Grumble Street." Possessed of a new spirit, he declared, "Since I became a Christian, I moved out on Thanksgiving Street."

Some have become so fed up with the dollar sign, the piling

up of things, the glamour of success, they have lost appreciation
for everything. Billy Graham told of a famous film star who
exclaimed, "I have money, beauty, popularity, but I am miserable." A prominent man said, "I have lost all desire to live, yet
I have everything to live for." A patient confided to his doctor,
"I am lonely, despondent, miserable." A college student moaned,
"I am already fed up with life."

In contrast, think how grateful the Founding Fathers of our
nation were to be alive, free, and with something to eat. They
faced the perils of the sea, and danger and death in the untamed
wilderness, with the spirit of thanksgiving and dauntless courage.

Coming closer to our time, a blind, bedridden preacher con-
ducted a radio program that brought good news and cheer to
many listeners. Far from disheartened, he announced, "Thank
God, my anchor holds." As his condition grew worse, he continued, "I can no longer move, but I can pray and praise God."
Happiness hinges more on the inner spirit than on outward
circumstances.

4. The deeper satisfactions of life come to us in the spiritual
rewards of sharing and service. "One thing I know," said Dr.
Albert Schweitzer; "the only ones among you who will be really
happy are those who have sought and found how to serve."

Another man, Frank Laubach, brought much joy to under-
privileged people. "When people discover for the first time they
can read," he said, "men become hysterical and women leap for
joy." The apostle of learning found his greatest happiness in
doing something for others.

No one who lives wholly inside himself can find happiness.
As Roy L. Smith said, "Until we have learned to live outside
ourselves, we have not really learned to live at all."

A preacher decided to write a letter of encouragement to a
stranger whose name he had read in the morning paper. The
next day he decided to do it again. This became a habit with
him. As he read the paper in the morning, he found some person
in trouble or who had been honored, and wrote a cheering word
or a note of appreciation. A simple deed of helpfulness brought
an inner joy and spiritual glow for the entire day.

There are spiritual rewards of satisfaction and joy in self-giving and sharing. "Rejoice and be exceeding glad," Christ said, "for your reward is great in heaven."

READ: Psalm 33:1–5; Philippians 4:4

PRAYER: May we know, O Lord, that real happiness comes to those who have found the deeper meaning of life in Thee. Amen.

9 THE LIFT OF QUIET MOMENTS

The story is told of the man who sprinted madly to catch a bus. Lunging through the door and stumbling up the steps, he staggered to his seat, panting and exhausted. Composing himself a bit, he stuttered as he turned to a fellow passenger, "Hey-uh, where—where is this bus going?"

We are in a fast-moving generation, so we must step lively to stay with the hurried procession. But we need to slow down for our health and well-being, and for the sake of our souls.

Growth, maturity, education, and expansiveness of the spirit, require time. There are no short cuts for the larger completion or perfection of life. God is not in a hurry. The psalmist caught the spirit of the Eternal: "He leads me beside the still waters, he restores my soul."

Consider the mood of the modern era. We somehow admire a busy man who is always dashing off to keep an appointment. But a recent book pokes fun at us by describing a man who used two shaving brushes instead of one and saved seventeen seconds. Another morning he used two razors instead of one and saved additional time. On a third day, however, he lost two minutes in patching up his chin after it had been sliced by the second razor. As someone commented, "Blessed is he who goeth around in circles."

Weakness of body and barrenness of mind and spirit are too typical of the age. Some two centuries ago Pascal wrote, "All the evils of modern life have fallen upon us because men will not sit alone quietly."

The famous historian H. G. Wells lamented the invasion of his time with minor matters and cluttered-up affairs. "My hours are choked with them," he wrote. "My thoughts are tattered with them. The clock ticks on, the moments drip out and trickle, flow away as hours." But Wells knew how to lop off the unessentials and to center his attention on worthful things.

It's not how fast we move that is significant, but the purpose and direction of our lives, the quality of our work. When his immortal painting "The Last Supper" was being done, Leonardo da Vinci spent hours in meditation. Some felt he was wasting time and fouling up the contract, but he replied, "When I pause the longest, I make the most telling strokes with my brush."

We must learn to relax, to let go. Some are like the man who was persuaded to take a flight in an airplane. Landing on the airstrip, the man was tense, and with clinched hands he murmured, "I never let my weight down."

A physician advised a patient to take an extended trip. The man visited several places in another state, and put much wear on his car and some on himself. When he came home he was still nervous, confused, and frustrated.

The need for living without stress and strain was pointed up some years ago by Owen Murphy, who opened a factory to make relaxing machines. Ten years later he had five plants and a payroll of twenty-five million dollars annually.

But there are more natural and normal ways of relaxing. The psalmist found healing moments out in the open spaces, beside the still streams and under the starry heavens. He found "the world is such a lovely place, sea, sky, and sod, since I have learned to live in peace and unity with God."

Vacations are an accepted pattern of our day. "But the devil never takes a vacation," Harry E. Fosdick was told. "That's the reason he's the devil," quipped Dr. Fosdick. "I would be like the devil, too, if I didn't take a vacation," he added.

A daily schedule may help to ease our burden. "For everything there is a season, and a time for every matter under heaven," wrote the ancient philosopher. There is wisdom in the timing of our work and leisure. One thing at a time, and we may have a grateful feeling that we have both labor and leisure moments.

The need for relaxing also stresses the importance of renewing our strength. There should be a wheel of balance between the expending of our energies and the intake of strength.

The human machine, like a motor, needs tuning up and refueling. We need rest and recreation. We need periods of creative waiting when we are responsive to new insights and receive the inspiration of mind and soul.

A football player occasionally breaks into the open field and dashes toward the goal with a burst of power to win for his team in the closing seconds of the game. The star of the game seems to have an invasion of strength outside himself. Such feats are made possible by the storing up of energy in periods of training and preparation for the great moments.

Bishop Everett W. Palmer told what it meant to live by the broad beaches of the Atlantic. The sea roared, the cars and buses buzzed by, and footsteps clattered on the sidewalks. But when the traffic was stilled and the strident voices were hushed in slumber, Bishop Palmer heard the mighty organ of the deep and the awesome music of unbroken rhythm. God was "closer than breathing, nearer than hands and feet."

Spiritual disciplines, devotional periods, should be observed with the family group and alone every day. "Come apart," Christ urged his disciples, and the moments quivered with meaning as they waited in silence in the presence of God.

Quiet, thoughtful moments should give us spiritual resources and make us adequate for any experience. When John Oxenham was informed that his son was killed in World War I, he wandered down the street alone with the burden of his sorrow. Staggering into a nearby chapel, he found peace for his soul.

There, in the deepening twilight, he wrote the words that found their way into our hymn book:

> 'Mid all the traffic of the ways,
> Turmoils without, within,
> Make in my heart a quiet place
> And come and dwell therein.

READ: Lamentations 3:22–28; Isaiah 40:28–31

PRAYER: "Slow me down, Lord. Ease the pounding of my heart by the quieting of my mind. Slow me down to look at a flower, to chat with a friend, to pat a dog, to read a few lines from a good book." Amen. (*An old prayer. Anon.*)

10   *WHEN GOD IS REAL TO US*

Most people feel that religion is a respectable thing and that everybody should belong to the church. But does it vitally affect our lives? "The great liability of Christianity is public approval without private faith," wrote Halford E. Luccock. So, with Easter there is much public approval, but the occasion lacks something in dynamic faith and personal experience of the living Christ. As Paul said, "Last of all . . . he appeared also to me."

Isn't much of religion casual and complacent? We take it for granted without getting through to a personal experience and feeling its reality.

Words spoken in the worship service may slip through our lips or fall upon our ears without meaning. We have heard them or spoken them so often that they fail to register with us.

Do we feel as the man of old: "Surely God is in this place," or "Woe is me, for I am an undone [sinful] man"?

Vital religion is a feeling or awareness of the indwelling spirit and power of God. A person who had been a member of the church for years seemed to come alive with a new experience. "I hadn't felt anything," he stated, "until something happened to me in that meeting." It appeared that God became more meaningful to the worshipper.

The year 1963 marked the 225th anniversary of John Wesley's Aldersgate experience. What seemed a too conventional, outward religion exploded for Wesley in a street prayer meeting. "I felt my heart strangely warmed," Wesley described the experience. The event "changed his weakness into power, his frustration into assurance," wrote Bishop Gerald Kennedy. From that time a freshness, enthusiasm, and power marked his preaching.

A breakthrough in religion was experienced by Job. In a time of disillusionment, suffering, and sorrow he found that a casual religion would not do. Driven to the deeper resources of God, he discovered adequacy in religion. "I had heard of thee by hearsay, but now mine eyes have seen thee," Job declared.

He journeyed in religion from rumor to reality, from pretense to power. "In his fellowship with God he had found that nothing matters in comparison with that fellowship. The man who has found fellowship with God is rich though he possesses nothing," said William Temple.

As I worshipped in a magnificent sanctuary somes years ago the organ music and lighting effects made a deep impression upon me. Like Jacob of old, I felt like shouting, "Surely God is in this place!"

Consider that God is most real to us when we have fellowship with Him and are obedient to His will. I was told of two women who had been shopping and were on the sidewalk, laden with packages. Their visibility obscured, they bumped into each other. One of the women screamed, "Why don't you look where you're going?" The other exclaimed, "Why don't you go where you are looking?" Many clashes occur because the vision of God is dimmed, and the sense of direction is confused.

If we are to do the will of God for us, we must have a feeling of His presence, and follow on the Way. A little girl told how Enoch walked with the Lord. "God and Enoch took

long walks together," she said. "One day they walked farther
than usual. So the Lord spoke: Enoch, you must be tired. Come
into my Father's house and rest."

Are our purposes and plans in harmony with the Lord? Are
we walking in the same direction? A troubled man went to a
pastor with a problem situation. After listening to the confused
man for some time, the minister asked, "Do you really want a
change in your life? If so, you must do God's will rather than
your own. You must turn your life over to God and make a
break with your past."

For some the reality of God is more apparent in a crisis. I
recall the visit of an electrician some years ago who told of his
bout with a live wire and of his brush with death. He was so
shaken up emotionally, he resolved to make a new beginning
with God and the church, for he "had drifted away," as he
described his complacency.

A somewhat different experience was related by Robert
Louis Stevenson, who told of a storm that rocked his ship and
threatened the lives of all aboard near one of the South Sea
Islands. Fear-possessed, the men huddled in a cabin. Meanwhile,
one of the men ventured out on deck and saw the captain of
the ship walking to and fro, calmly and confidently.

Returning to the frightened men in the cabin, he said, "I have
seen the face of the captain and all is well." Amid the disturbing
and distressing experiences of life, the psalmist gives us the
assurance, "God is our refuge and strength, a very present help
in trouble."

As we turn the pages of the Bible, we find that God was
very real to the prophets, especially in times of adversity. In
the turn of historic events Isaiah was sensitive to spiritual and
eternal values. He described in symbolism his awareness of the
divine presence, and His cleansing power and call.

One other step in spiritual reality is concern and compassion
for our fellow men. No one can be on intimate terms with God
unless he has love in his heart for others. "He who loves his
brother abides in the light."

An old story is told of the shoemaker who looked for the

coming of Christ to his humble home. As he was reading the Bible one day, he heard a voice: "Martin, look for me tomorrow on the street." But the next day Martin looked in vain for the Christ.

When a soldier came into the shop, the cobbler gave him a cup of warm tea. Somewhat later a woman with a child came in, shivering from the bitter cold. Martin gave them warm food, clothing, and money. That evening, as the twilight darkened, the shoemaker had a vision of Christ and heard the voice: "Inasmuch as you have done it unto one of the least of these, you have done it unto me." Where love is expressed in being a brother in need, there is God.

God is real to us when we have a sense of His presence, and are outgoing in our love to others. As someone said, "I find myself in finding God."

READ: Isaiah 6:1–9, 61:1–2
PRAYER: Come close to us, O Christ, and make thy Presence real this day. "Breathe on us breath of God, till we are wholly Thine." In the spirit of Christ. Amen.

11   *WHEN TROUBLE COMES*

At an annual church conference a handicapped reporter did a good job of covering the sessions. Leaning on a crutch, he bent almost double when he walked, and dragged his feet. Holding the paper close to his eyes, he wrote in large script. There was no self-pity. He simply did his assignment in the face of heavy handicaps.

Mental attitudes have a direct effect on the body. A disturbing thought brings a blush to the cheek. An unpleasant incident may blunt the appetite or upset the night's rest. Morbid thoughts slow down the function of the body, while happy thoughts give a glow and tingle.

A study of the common headache, which may reflect a state of the mind, revealed that 65 per cent of our people regularly have headaches. Single persons have more headaches than married ones. People of a tense, emotional disposition have more trouble than those of a calm and cheery mood.

Three ways of handling our handicaps were mentioned by Robert E. Goodrich, Jr.: (1) we can dispose of them or set them aside; (2) we may take each problem or day at the time; (3) we may share our problems with others.

In the first place, we may be carrying needless loads of anxieties that have no foundation in fact. To do that we may need some wise counseling or a commitment of our lives to Christ. A young man went through a clinic, which discovered no physical maladies. Turned over to a psychiatrist, he was told, "What you need is work, not worry." When he grasped that fact he forgot his anxieties and got busy on his vocation.

The distress of many people in this nuclear age is borne out by a woman who said, "I am worried to death. A war may come and we have no air-raid shelter to protect us from a fallout."

During a period of falling stars many feared that the world was coming to an end. Among the panicky people, however, was an old, saintly Negro who looked upward and said, "Only the little stars are falling. See those great big stars—dey haven't moved one inch." God is still in charge of the universe, he felt, and our lives are in His hands.

Trouble in the form of guilt may pile up inside of us, and bear us down. Consider a woman who came to a pastor and unburdened her heart after interviews with psychiatrists. Together they prayed, asking the forgiveness of God. Relieved of her sense of guilt, she experienced a feeling of joy and peace. So burdens of fear and worry may be set aside.

A second way of dealing with life's situations is to take each problem or day as it comes. In moving, for instance, we do not place all the dishes, books, and other household articles on the van at once, but pack the items in cartons so they can be handled a bit at a time. So the load of life may be broken into fragments and carried a bit at a time.

Or we may keep in mind that time is broken up into minutes, hours, and days. In old *McGuffey's Reader*, as the story goes, an ancient clock stopped. It was disheartened because of the thought of the number of seconds it must tick in the course of a year—some thirty-two million. When it dawned on the clock it had to tick only one second at a time, it began to run again. The lesson is plain; let each moment and day be content with its problems and exciting experiences.

In his widely read book *Out of the Night*, Jan Valtin told of being sentenced as a war prisoner to some ten years. The future seemed to him dark and forbidding. But he learned to bear his burden by his resolve to live only one day at a time. By concentrating on each day as it unfolded, he endured his experiences and wrote a famous book that was very rewarding to him.

Fortunately we cannot see the long road ahead. Nor does God lay the full weight of life on our shoulders, but a little each day. No matter how heavy the load, or how deep the pathway, we can go on, if by God's strength we only bear the burden of the hour.

The third way to face trouble is to share our problem. Emotions bottled up within us may break out in physical, mental, and nervous maladies.

A prominent man, with an evident feeling of failure and frustration among mounting responsibilities, took his own life. One of his friends remarked that he had intended talking to the man. Had the distressed man bared his soul to his understanding, sympathetic friend, he might have lived usefully for many years.

One of the heavest burdens we sometimes carry is that of discouragement. The legend is told of the devils in hell who were discussing means of placing obstacles in the path of man.

Many tools for man's undoing were kicked around . . . deceit, perfidy, theft. Then one of the demons spoke of one of the sharpest and deadliest instruments, discouragement.

Hobbies and outside interests can be of great help in standing up under difficulties and handicaps. A woman who had been confined to the hospital for years exclaimed, "I am shut in but not out." She added, "I am interested in football, baseball, music, politics, religion." So, despite her crippled limbs and twisted hands, she lived happily and usefully.

Life may be zestful, too, if we enjoy the companionship of books. Robert Louis Stevenson looked upon books as the greatest remedy for his physical handicap. And they provide other sources of joy to lighten our load. As John Masefield wrote:

> London has been my prison; but my books
> Hills and great waters, laboring men and brooks,
> Ships and deep friendships and remembered days
> Which even now set all my mind ablaze.

("Biography," from his poems, Macmillan.)

But our deepest troubles will have to be solved by sharing them with and surrendering them to God. Healing power in illness, even to the extent of 90 per cent, is contributed by God, said Dr. R. C. Cabot. Doctors are but instruments in the hands of God and share 10 per cent of the healing process, he felt. Much of the ministry of our Lord was devoted to healing, and to helping in time of trouble.

READ: Psalm 46:1–11
PRAYER: Be a present help, O Lord, along the way of life and give us the assurance of Thy Presence and peace. Amen.

Vast throngs head toward the beaches on week ends and in the holiday seasons. During the time we lived in Dare County, North Carolina, we, too, felt the thrill of the lash of the waves, the lift of the tides, the lure of far horizons.

Here we heard stories of seafaring men, and were taken in by the saga and lore of the coast land. Tales were told of a dog that rescued a crew; of cannibalism at sea; of the hurricane that tore up the seas and tossed nine vessels upon the beach; and of the only known case of childbirth in a lifeboat.

The "Lost Colony" drama enacted every summer on Roanoke Island since 1937 has drawn thousands of people to the coast land, and injected new life into a sleeping community, once shut off from the world.

Seeing the famous production, the dream and sacrifices of the Founding Fathers come alive, we are stirred by their courage and their commitment to the way of freedom.

Consider the lash of the winds and waves that are carrying away the sands and changing the shore lines, moving millions of tons of soil.

Standing on Cape Hatteras on a stormy day, we may watch the awesome display of savage fury. Here the warm Gulf Stream meets the cold currents coming down from the Arctic, and they run head-on into each other, tossing their spume a hundred feet into the air, and dropping sand, shells, and sea life.

There is a familiar story of the daring of Coast Guards who went to the aid of a distressed ship when a northeaster churned up the sea. The captain ordered the men to go at once to the rescue of the stricken ship.

"Sir," exclaimed one of the men, "we can go out, but against the wind and waves we cannot come back." The captain barked,

"Our regulations don't say a —— thing about coming back. We've got to go out."

Even as the winds and waves beat upon the shores, so man is tested by the adverse circumstances of life.

When the noted Scottish entertainer and singer Sir Harry Lauder lost his only son in World War I, he said to a friend, "When a man comes to a thing like this, there are just three ways out of it: there is drink, there is despair, and there is God. By His grace it's God for me."

A man in chains was on his way to Rome. "A tempestuous wind, called the northeaster, struck down from the land," said Paul. The hero of the hour stilled the fears of a near-panicky people, crying: "So take heart, for I have faith in God." We, too, may find adequacy in a vital faith.

The lift of the tides may suggests the resources of God available to us. Consider that the total volume of the seas is 324 cubic miles, fourteen times the volume of dry land above sea level. How tremendous, then, is the power of the tides!

In building Hell Gate Bridge over the East River in New York, engineers discovered an abandoned ship embedded in the mud at the bottom of the stream. The obstacle had to be removed so that the central pier could go down for a solid footing. All initial atempts to budge the derelict vessel were futile.

Then a huge flatboat, used to haul rock downstream, was towed into position. Chaining it to the sunken ship at low tide, the men waited for the great volume of water to sweep in from the ocean, with all the power of the sea behind it. The old craft was lifted as the tide came in, inch by inch until ready to be towed out and dropped into the bosom of the ocean. This story brings to our minds the unfathomed resources of God, which we may lay hold on.

In our catastrophic world, as General Omar Bradley said, "Our knowledge of science has clearly outstripped our capacity to control it. We have men of science, too few men of God," he continued. "We have grasped the mystery of the atom and rejected the Sermon on the Mount. We have nuclear giants and ethical infants."

The far view of the sea reminds us we no longer live on little islands, but are linked indissolubly with the peoples of the world, even as the waters wash the shores of all continents.

The vision and outreach of men are often too limited, or confined within the circle of family or group, unconcerned about the great world beyond. Men who take out fishing parties have some helpful advice for us. "Stop looking at the end of your pole against the moving waters," they tell us; "look off toward the horizon." We need the large view of concern and compassion for all men.

With the Christian outlook on life, the boundary lines of nations and races are overleaped. The unguarded border of the United States and Canada witnesses the power of neighborliness and mutual concern. If all nations had the far view, the Christian way of seeing each other, barriers of fear and distrust would fall away.

READ: Psalm 93

PRAYER: Still our unquiet hearts, O Master of the seas and of life. Give us strength, steadfastness, and the far-seeing vision in our relationship to others. In Christ's name. Amen.

13 *HELP FROM THE HILLS*

Some thirty miles southwest of Asheville, North Carolina, Lake Junaluska nestles among the hills to form a magnificent setting for the Summer Assembly of Methodism's Southeastern Jurisdiction. No spot could be more suitable and inspiring for spiritual adventuring, or for rest and renewal of body and spirit.

Standing at a large cross at the summit, one has a commanding view of the lake and the surrounding hills. At night the cross is lighted and can be seen from many homes and hotels. The cross was once blacked out, and the railroad men, winding down the mountain trail some hours before dawn, sorely missed the illuminated cross, the story goes. From the lighted cross gleamed an inner glow of cheer and courage during the weary hours of night. Then the trainmen started a petition and pledged their support for the continuance of the bright symbol of Calvary.

During their vacation a pastor and his wife spent some stimulating and memorable days at Lake Junaluska. Then they wound over the hills from the Great Smokies to Roanoke, Virginia, traversing the famous Blue Ridge Parkway, beholding some of the most breath-taking scenery in the world.

Landmarks of another day were seen. Old log cabins, where generations of mountain folk dwelt in deep isolation, still stand. A grist mill, driven by waterpower, is one of the most striking sights along the modern thoroughfare. A huge wooden wheel, turned by flowing water, and heavy grinding stones are the outstanding features of the mill.

But this narrative is not simply a travelogue. What is the message that echoes from the hills?

The flame of life may blaze anew upon the mountaintop. In the lowlands the vision of life may grow dim and our hopes fade. The look to the hills may break the deadly routine, and moments may quiver with meaning for us.

A man, weary of the grind of life, gave a description of his week-by-week round of duties. He spelled out the monotony: going to the same office, riding the same elevator, hanging his coat in the same closet, seeing the same faces and doing the same work, in the same way. What a stale and stifling atmosphere!

A girl found some relief from her work by taking a mental and spiritual break during the day. She went to the window in a towering building, letting her eyes linger on the far horizon, spending moments in meditation and drinking in the beauty of the distant scenery.

As for me, I had a thrilling experience in the journey over the mountains. It was a shining hour. I parked at times high over

the mountain wall, and stood in awe and reverence. God seemed
to come very close to me and to be very real.

"Trust your high moments," someone said. Let not the vision
be tarnished nor the goal lost from view. Let no doubt and
darkness overtake us, but keep the flaming soul.

Spiritual leaders have had much of their schooling in the
quietness of the hill country. Isaiah caught a vision of the nations
flowing to the mountain of God, seeking to learn of his ways
and to walk in his path. In days of testing and sore trial, Paul
bore witness before Agrippa: "I was not disobedient to the
heavenly vision." In days of quiet study and meditation God's
grace had made him strong.

In a journey over the Blue Ridge Parkway, I saw one of the
oldest mountains in the world, Grandfather Mountain. The
green graying rocks date from prehistoric times, millions of
years, it is believed. So on the hills we catch the long view of
time and eternity.

Young men are noted for their enthusiasm and courage.
They look ahead and are not slaves to the past.

But age is not bound by the calendar. Our senior citizens
today are rapidly growing in numbers. As retired men and
women, millions have found new things to do and new potentialities in life. They are neither lazy nor licked.

They are in the noble company of Caleb, who at eighty-five
years of age was alive and alert to his fingertips. "Now, therefore," Caleb prayed, "give me this mountain." He would lead
out in conquering a new world, in doing what some felt impossible. "Let us go up at once and possess the land," Caleb cried.

Observe, too, I was confronted with the peace and eternity
of God in our trek over the mountains. Bishop Quayle spoke
of how "we valley dwellers grow wearied, and our eyeballs
ache . . . but unperturbed quietness rests upon the hill."

The hills are the spires that lift men's thoughts upward, the
graceful symbols of the unseen and eternal. So elevation of the
body gives us some elevation of thought. Our minds hark back
to summit, spiritual retreats, and moments of silence and awe as
the rising sun steeps the world in beauty, seen from the hilltops.

We face the need for a universal language for all mankind. Fortunately we do have a common medium of communication as we lift our eyes to the hills that speak of the unseen and eternal. The pride, arrogance, and self-sufficiency of man will have their little day, but the mountains remind us of the eternity of God.

They give us a sense of God's presence and power over us. On the long journey to Jerusalem travelers encamped for the night among the hills of Palestine, centuries ago. During the darkness some stood guard to protect the pious pilgrims from robbers. Spiritually sensitive men, however, saw another guardian, the Lord, who neither slumbered nor slept.

> We travel the dusty road till the light of day is dim,
> And the sunset shows us spires away on the world's rim."
>
> (*Masefield, "The Seekers"*)

READ: Psalm 121

PRAYER: May we lift our eyes to the hills of God and live on the high level of the life in Christ. Amen.

14   *GETTING ALONG WITH PEOPLE*

A study was made some years ago to discover the most serious blunders young people make in their first jobs. In an inquiry of several thousand businessmen, the survey found that two-thirds of the young men lost their first positions because they couldn't get along with people.

"The secret of success and happiness is determined in large measure by your ability to get along with other people," commented John H. Miller.

Consider the personal nature of friendship. To his disciples Jesus said, "I have called you friends." He used the figure of the "good shepherd" to reveal his warmth and personal concern for people.

I cherish memories of a college friend, George W. McDaniel, long-time pastor of First Baptist Church, Richmond, Virginia. Visiting the campus of the University of Richmond, he encouraged the students in their college activities and hopes for the future. He called me by name and seemed never too busy to take a personal interest in me.

As a judge told Theodore Roosevelt, "You never talk five minutes with any man without making him believe you like him very much." The clasp of the hand, the twinkle of the eye, the glow of the face, the conversation, all may betray a friendly concern for people.

The noted psychologist William James once had a long and serious illness. Someone sent him a potted azalea, along with some friendly words. Touched by the gesture of kindness, James wrote, "The deepest quality of human nature is the craving for appreciation."

A friend may be the key to the beginning of a new life. A pastor once talked to a teenager who was part of a group charged with a "break-in." The community was aroused over the deed and some hard things were said about the youth. But as the minister confronted him, the boy acknowledged his fault and showed the spirit of repentance for his part in the misdeed. "It will never happen again," the young man moaned.

In the words of James Whitcomb Riley:

> When a man ain't got a cent,
> An' he's feeling kind of blue,
> An' the clouds hang dark and heavy,
> An' won't let the sunshine through,
> It's a great thing, oh my brother,
> For a feller just to lay
> His hand upon your shoulder
> In a friendly sort of way.

To make and keep friendships, we must learn to differ without being angry. While people have different ideas on controversial issues, no one has the perfect answer. As friends we must be able to disagree and still love each other.

The pastor of a large church delivered a message on race relations. At the close of his sermon he reminded his people of his love for them and of his concern for his country. No one seemed to object to the words spoken in love and on the basis of the scriptures.

"We are to bear one another's burdens." The Bible accents the need of spending oneself for others, without counting the cost. A real friend will give and give, and even lay down his life to save his friend.

To bear one another's burdens, we must go beyond the thought of mere financial aid, important as that may be. Tolstoy not only spent his savings for the poor, but continued to feel deeply for them.

One day he met a beggar who asked aid. Reaching in his pocket, he found no change to give the man. He walked up to the poor man, wrapped his arms around him and said, apologetically: "Do not be angry with me, little brother, because I have nothing to give you." The beggar was moved by such words of affection, and mumbled as tears ran down his cheeks, "But, sir, you call me brother; that was a great gift."

The classic story of Damon and Pythias points up the value of friendships. As the story goes, a young man displeased the king and was sentenced to die. When he was imprisoned, he asked the ruler for permission to pay a final visit to his family, who lived some distance away. The king laughed at the request, feeling it was a scheme to escape.

Then the young man Damon came up and urged the king to let the prisoner go, offering to take his place in prison or to be executed. Impressed by such a strange offer of sacrifice, he allowed Pythias to go. Weeks passed and Pythias did not return as expected. The friend was led out to pay the supreme price for another. At that moment a cloud of dust appeared in the distance, and Pythias was coming back in great haste, having been delayed by earthquake and storm.

Pythias prepared to die, but the king stayed the hand of the executioner, saying, "I would give all that I possess if I had one such friend."

Though our friends and loved ones may be out of sight, they should not be out of our minds and hearts. Communications, simple letters or cards, or telephone calls should keep them mindful of our concern.

A father wrote his son across the seas, "I am hanging a prayer on every star for you." When the boy glanced up at the stars at night, he knew his father was praying for him to keep steady and strong.

"I have called you friends," Christ told the disciples. "Love one another as I have loved you."

READ: John 15:12–17

PRAYER: Give us understanding and good will, O Lord, for one another. Bind together Thy children in the bonds of Christian love, and fill our hearts with the joy of fellowship. Amen.

15 *AS THE YEARS GO BY*

Our chances of living longer on earth are far better than they were for our ancestors. By 1980 we are expected to have more than twenty-two million people in our country over sixty-five years of age. With continued development of medical science and health measures, life expectancy will probably reach 91.1 years by 2020.

Now what will these added years means for us? They can

be either a bane or a blessing, a bore or a boon. A woman hospital patient complained of living so long. But when she returned home with the glow of health, she had a song in her heart.

A doctor told one of his patients he could live years longer if he would exercise moderation in his habits. But he had grown weary in the mere succession of days.

It's important that we get ready for tomorrow. The obvious way of preparing for the coming years is to live well and wisely today. Some people speak of writing books when they retire, but some of those volumes must be created in the present. We may consider life a stream that flows on toward the ocean of eternity, not as new springs of inspiration that gush out in later years.

As the years go by we must make some adjustments for the body's sake. Writing of "Eighty Adventurous Years," Sherwood Eddy told how he developed a heart condition by straining himself. He tried to force his voice to speak under difficult circumstances, and felt a sharp pain. One day he struggled with some heavy luggage, and had a second heart attack. So he learned to take mild exercise and never to drive himself out of breath, nor to hurry and worry.

But as the physical limitations grow apace as the years go by, the mind and spirit need not become dull, nor interest and friendship fade, nor life grow dim.

When John Adams was an old man, someone asked him about his state of health. He replied, "John Adams is fine—he is grateful, happy, busy." He added, "Though the house in which John Adams lives is falling apart . . . John Adams is fine, thank you." As we have seen, the physical man lasts longer today. But what is more important is that we may continue to grow in deeper understanding, riper wisdom, patience, and poise.

We need to keep fresh and forward-looking in mind and spirit. While there are memories that linger and streams of joys that flow on, we need not be bound entirely to the past. A sixty-four-year-old man was asked if he was aware of the many changes that had taken place during the past fifty years. "Yes," he answered, "and I have been agin every dang one of them."

In the Bible we have the incident of the Hebrew people facing hardships and uncertainties in the wilderness. They became embittered and cried out against Moses, "Would that we had died . . . in the land of Egypt." Then Moses talked to the Lord about the mutiny of his people, and the answer came, "Tell the people of Israel to go forward" (Exod. 14). The way is ever forward, not backward.

To live fully in the present, we must keep growing. Even as a tree, we may grow a little new wood every year. One of the secrets of Theodore Roosevelt's greatness was his passion for study and his firm belief that one is never too old to acquire new knowledge.

Sherwood Eddy told in his autobiography of how in later years he slowed down in his public-speaking career, despite numerous requests. It gave him more time for reading and writing, he said.

At eighty-eight Frank Boyd, author of *The Fine Art of Living*, had the zest of a boy. Hard at work every day, he helped men and women renew their youth.

Recall the classic words of Tennyson:

> And this gray spirit yearning in desire,
> To follow knowledge like a sinking star,
> Beyond the utmost bounds of human thought.

Age and youth are affected more by attitudes than by arteries, we are informed. By changing the attitude of the mind, we can alter the outward aspects of our lives.

As the years go by we can think more in terms of service than of status. The illusions of youth have faded, and we have found new dimensions of reality in religion, a zest for old and new friendships, and a life of self-giving.

An aging much-loved teacher wrote notes or letters to his former students. He kept in touch with "the boys," and gave them encouragement. Hearing from him was like a telephone call or visit, for his words dripped with personal concern and affection. He was not unlike an elderly minister who told a friend that he felt his best contribution was made by the letters he had written.

On a warm, sultry afternoon in June, a ninety-year-old man was seen distributing some material for his church. "Surely," said a friend, "you ought not to be out this hot afternoon." Looking the younger man in the eye, the oldster replied, "When His Word says Go, that means every one of us, including me." While the old man might not have been prudent, he was still fired with a sense of purpose and passion to serve his fellow men.

Many older people yield to the lure of far horizons, and new worlds are opened for them through travel. Some of us have been thrilled with motor-coach tours through New England and Canada. Many tour the country in their own cars, while others globe-trot in this jet age.

Getting ready for adventures into places unkonwn to us will pay off. A man borrowed from the public library books on new lands for his explorations. Then he gathered material along the way, asked questions of natives, made extensive notes. When the trip was over, he wrote a story of his journey and shared it with others.

So, with new freedom to live and to serve after retirement, we should reassess life's values and readjust our schedule, then live zestfully, with a spiritual glow in our hearts.

As Henry van Dyke wrote:

> So let the way wind up hill or down,
> O'er rough or smooth, the journey will be joy;
> Still seeking what I sought when but a boy,
> New friendship, high adventure, and a crown,
> I shall grow old, but never lose life's zest,
> Because the road's last turn will be the best.

READ: Psalm 16, 92:14; Luke 12:15–21

PRAYER: We thank thee, O Lord, for the gift of life. As the years go by, help us to grow in wisdom, spiritual stature, and usefulness. Amen.

16   *WHEN THE LITTLE BECOMES MUCH*
(*Spirit of Giving*)

In writing the story of his life, Bronson Alcott made good use of red ink. What he regarded as important events were written in red: the birth of his daughter . . . the first robin in spring . . . the color of Concord trees in the fall. Giving a cup of cold water, Jesus assured us, could be big business and go down on the credit side.

The so-called little things are often overlooked. A retired man wrote a postal to a discouraged woman whose father was ill and whose husband was addicted to alcohol. "I want you to know I care and will pray for you," he wrote consolingly. Replying to his thoughtful card, she said, "Your message lifted my load . . . I read it several times during the day just to feel someone cared."

A smile, it seemed, saved a man's life. During the depression in 1933, a man who had lost his job sat on the banks of the Hudson River, thinking of leaping into the water. Suddenly he was startled to hear sirens from motorcycles leading a touring car with the top down.

Jumping to his feet, the man was just in time to see Franklin D. Roosevelt waving to him and cheering him by his famous smile. The despondent man headed back to his home state to establish a successful business. A little thing! A big meaning!

A little boy offered his lunch, and a hungry crowd was fed by Christ. Seeing the possibilities in children, Christ urged Peter, "Feed my lambs."

Consider for a moment, then, our responsibility to children in the church. Much has been written about drop-outs in school. More serious still are the drops-outs in church. Gathering in the harvest of members has not been too easy.

But one pastor told of how he magnified the meaning of church membership. Children were given twelve weeks of intensive training, both in groups and as individuals. Then, upon taking the first step to follow Christ, they were given attractive folders with instructions, and a responsible person was assigned to help each child grow in Christian grace. The individual was kept in mind and in heart, as the years unfolded.

Numbers have been overemphasized in the church because of flattering reports. I recall that only one lad was baptized in a certain church during the year. The members felt discouraged, and there were rumblings of the need for a new pastor. But the one new member received into the fellowship that year was Robert Moffatt, the man who achieved missionary fame.

Teamwork is essential for the greatest group impact. Star players thrill us in a football game, but the spectacular get-aways are made possible by good interference, faking, passing, the co-ordination and alertness of the entire team. The little becomes much when men function as an effective unit.

The scriptures stress the importance of everyone doing his best, utilizing his talent. Halford Luccock told of "dead money" in the banks, soaring to fifty million dollars. The unclaimed money had been deposited by over two million people. So money hoarded or misused may be termed dead money. Unfortunately there is not only unused or misused money; many talents are unharnessed for service of the Kingdom.

In the gospel the tragedy of neglect of the one-talent is played up, for it represents many of us today. A woman insisted she had no talents, and the pastor reminded her that her presence and her prayers were needed for the church.

Some people have the gift of the warm handclasp, of friendship. A boy left one church for another congregation. When asked about the swap, he replied, "I go to church where the people love me."

The "every one teach one" idea of Frank Laubach spread rapidly, and the light of learning went out to millions in undeveloped countries.

The story goes that a little girl went to a drugstore with twenty-five pennies in her hands and laid them down on the counter and told the clerk, "I want a miracle."

Surprised, the clerk asked, "What did you say?" The little girl answered, "I want a miracle." Chuckling, the clerk said, "I don't think we have one. What do you want a miracle for?"

Then the little girl related her story. "My brother is ill and I heard our doctor tell my mother, unless we could get Dr. Abernethy, only a miracle could save him." Then she told of how her parents didn't feel they could afford to have Dr. Abernethy. "So I opened my bank," she said, "and this is my money, and that's why I want to buy a miracle."

A man who happened to be in the store turned to the child, saying, "I'd like to go to your house. I'm Dr. Abernethy. Perhaps God will help us do that miracle for you."

The little may become much as God and man work together.

Often the silent and unnoticed influences are cumulative, creatively enriching and ennobling human life. The harvest follows on the heels of seed planting and cultivation.

Senator Frank Norris told of how his elderly mother planted a fruit tree in the yard. "Why," asked someone, "since you will not live to see fruit on that tree?" She replied, "But somebody else will."

The cult of bigness and noise need not mislead us. Great movements may grow silently out of small beginnings. Christianity emerged from far and faint beginnings to become earth's greatest benefit and blessing.

A lad helped to feed the throng of people. So the little may become much when committed to Christ.

READ: John 6:1–14

PRAYER: Make us faithful, O God, in the living of this day. May we not overlook the little things that may bring big blessings to others. In Christ's name. Amen.

(*Loyalty Sunday*)

One Sunday morning a woman arrived quite late for the worship service. Seeing the usher near the entrance, she inquired, "Is the service over?" He replied, "The worship is over, but the service is just begun." So our religion should not be left at church nor solely in the hands of the preacher, but be a matter of everyday living and service.

Today there is renewed emphasis on every church member being spiritually alive and alert. Retreats and conferences are held for laymen, and all are urged to share the burden of sinful men and world conditions.

Christianity began as a lay movement. Jesus, an unordained teacher and preacher, lashed out against the hollow, conventional, formal religion of his day. He raised his voice against "professionals" who made "long prayers to be seen of men." He did not hesitate to help and heal man even on the Sabbath.

His followers continued his ministry of healing, teaching, and preaching. They sought out others and told them about the Man in their midst. Philip came up with Nathaniel and said, "We have found him of whom Moses and the prophets wrote." Andrew found his brother Simon Peter and brought him to Christ.

Long before the day of the printing press, radio, and television, the early Christians were all aglow with the good news of hope, joy, and the assurance of the abundant, eternal life. They were "heralds of a passion."

No one is unimportant in the church, and everyone has time, ability, and money that can be shared. Someone told of an orchestra conductor who on one occasion stopped the concert and asked, "What has happened to the piccolo?" The smallest instrument in the orchestra had ceased to function, and that was immediately detected. The one-talent man was condemned by our Lord because he failed to use what had been entrusted to him. We are not responsible for the number of talents we have received in life but rather for the proper use of them.

The second thing to observe is that we are *workers* together with God (II Cor. 6:1). Real religion is not sporadic or static, but daily and dynamic. Consider that in a day the heart beats about 103,000 times and the blood travels in the arteries and veins up to the astounding distance of 168 million miles. Regular, systematic performance of the body makes life possible.

A man was handicapped by a badly strained wrist. The doctor remarked to the pastor, "I know how the church feels in not having the use of all its members." Everyone in the church can be an effective part of the spiritual organism.

We once had sitdown strikes in certain factories, and the plants could not operate until the men stood on their feet and began to work. The Bible stresses the urgency of being alert and alive in the church.

Our vows in the church include the promise to be present for worship, to participate in the services, and to be paying or giving members. We should put our money to work for the causes of the Kingdom. But there is much unused and uncommitted money.

There is a remarkable story in the Bible of the able, patriotic leader Nehemiah, who grieved over the plight and suffering of his fellow Hebrews and the ruins of the ancient capital of Jerusalem. With zeal and a high sense of mission, he led some of his fellow countrymen back to rebuild the wall around the city. The people set to work—some stood guard, some lifted the stones, some placed them in position. Working from dawn until the stars came out at night, the wall was rebuilt in the incredibly short time of fifty-two days. The secret of their success? "The people had a mind to work" (Neh. 4:6).

Effective work is done in cooperation with others. We may be a good person apart from the church, as someone said, but not a Christian. Certainly when we join our strength with others, we magnify our influence and enable the church to make greater strides in the world community.

A child was once lost in a wide wheat field of Kansas. Neighbors hunted frantically for the little girl but were frustrated in their search. Then someone suggested they join hands and tramp through the grain field. In this way the child was soon found. If we are to have better understanding and cooperation with the peoples of the world, we must act together in many areas within the framework of the church.

We may also think of the church in terms of a team, disciplined and playing together as a unit and in loyalty to the institution. The coach, even as a pastor, trains and directs the group. But the success of the team is made possible by everyone doing his level best, taking his full part.

Today the burden of carrying the program should not be left entirely to the preacher. Some hundred million church members who live and work at their religion could turn the world "right side up." While the pastor is in charge of the church, the members are the church's link with the community and the world.

We are workers together *with God*. Not only ministers, but laymen, feel they are called of God. Some are called to teach, some to the healing ministry, some to counseling. . .

A judge of a juvenile court told of his concern for youth who got into trouble. Far from wreaking vengeance on the young people, he sought to help, to heal them of infection that had gotten into the moral blood stream.

The common tasks, too, can be by divine appointment. An orderly in a hospital for the aged and incurable had a personal concern for his patients. In his compassion he brought good cheer into the sickroom, and did his humble work with dignity and efficiency.

We are called to a life of service in fellowship with others. The question is not simply what the church can do for us, but what we can do for the church and its glorious ministry.

Remember: we are not merely going to church, but *are* the church in the world. "We are workers together with God."

READ: Romans 12:4–8
PRAYER: We rejoice, O Lord, in the privilege of being workers together with Thee. May we be found faithful in the use of our time, ability, and means. In Christ's name. Amen.

18   WHAT IS SUCCESS?

(Pre-Easter Message)

"Success" is often on the lips of young people. College students vote on the boy or girl most likely to succeed. Older people not only want to make a living, they wish to attain a good standing among their fellows. The successful man is regarded as one who becomes wealthy, prominent, powerful, one who achieves status in society.

A higher concept of success appears in the New Testament. When James and John were seeking top places in an earthly Kingdom, Jesus asked them if they were willing to drink his cup of self-giving and sacrifice. The mature life should be outgoing and sharing.

Success standards must be re-evaluated. The Christian criterion of success is giving rather than getting; a God-centered rather than a self-centered life.

Consider the young seamstress, Sadie, who lived in a small Virginia town. Ignored by the prominent people of the community, she became upset and embittered. To show the important people that she could succeed, she dreamed of saving her pennies

and taking a trip to Europe. At long last she saved enough
money to take her voyage across the seas.

But World War I broke out, and she was trapped in Belgium.
She was forced to return home. Her driver missed the road to
the port of embarkation and she found herself on the battlefield.

As the car stopped, Sadie heard a soldier crying, "Water,
water! For God's sake, water!" Leaping from the car, she found
water and gave it to the dying man. Then she went from one
soldier to another, offering a drink to parched lips, binding up
wounds, scribbling farewell notes to the people back home.

After that experience Sadie was no longer concerned about
making the "first families" list. Facing death, the horrors of hell,
nothing mattered now but "God and love, and doing things for
folks," she said. She discovered that successful living didn't mean
social status so much as commitment to the service of God and
man.

A sense of purpose is paramount in success. While Jesus
approved the aspiration of the human spirit, he wanted men to
go up higher and seek real greatness.

We esteem energy, initiative, ambition, ability—worthy quali-
ties provided they are headed in the right direction and are
intended to serve Christian ideals. In a novel, *Room at the Top*,
Joe Lampton is seen scheming and elbowing his way to the
top of the ladder of success, pushing others down in his upward
reach. A self-centered life may be very mercenary and ruthless.

Nor does greatness consists solely in things, as Jesus pointed
out. It is to have what Robert McCracken called a Distinguished
Service Cross, the spirit of self-giving.

Pity the man who thinks only in terms of possessions. Bishop
Everett Palmer told the story of a bachelor farmer in the Middle
West who advertised for a wife. "I am thirty-eight years old,"
he wrote. "Would like to marry young woman of thirty who
has tractor. Please send picture of tractor."

But life is to be organized with the conscious thought of
God at the center, with the feeling of purpose or mission in life.
We are "workers together with God." We are here to make the
highest contribution for the highest good of mankind.

James and John sought leadership without counting the cost in responsibility, anxiety, and involvement. They wanted the honor and prestige without the cross.

Some assume a detached attitude toward their fellows. Some years ago workmen were digging a ditch that suddenly caved in. When one of the spectators was told that his brother was caught under the landslide, he grabbed a tool and began to work frantically. As followers of Christ, should we not be concerned with the needs and hurts of all men?

When the Hebrew people were taken into captivity, Ezekiel went along with his people and shared their hardships. As the record states, "He sat where they sat." Too many show little concern for those who suffer today because of poverty, racial tension, or natural causes.

An elderly man was sitting on a bench in a city park one day when a student sat down beside him. Turning to the old man, the student asked, "What is your name? My name is ———." That was the first time, according to the old fellow, that anyone seemed to care enough to ask his name. It was a little thing, but it seemed to give him a new lease on life.

As Boris Pasternak wrote in his novel *Dr. Zhivago,* "Don't manipulate life; live it. Immerse yourself . . . in deep involvement with your fellow men."

The spirit of Christian vocation also adds new meaning and thrust to life. The story goes that a little girl was just beginning a study of arithmetic, and had learned about the plus sign. Attending church with her father one Sunday, she asked as she observed a cross, "Why do they have a plus sign in the church?" The cross is at the center of the Christian religion. It is a plus sign in our way of life.

So the early disciples had to learn of the deeper meaning of life from the teachings of Christ, the adversities of persecution, and the cross. Life was lifted to a higher level of self-giving, involvement, and Christian vocation.

"At the close of life," wrote N. C. Schaeffer, "the question will not be how much you have got, but how much you have given; not how much you have won, but how much you have done; not have much you have saved, but how much you have sacrificed."

READ: Matthew 20:20–28

PRAYER: Deliver us, heavenly Father, from vain desires and selfish aims. May we know that successful living and true greatness consist in commitment to Thy will. In Christ's name. Amen.

19 THIS IS LIFE ETERNAL
(*Easter Sunday*)

"I don't care what they say with their mouths—everybody knows something is eternal," said one of Thornton Wilder's characters in *Our Town*. "And it ain't houses . . . and it ain't earth, and it ain't even the stars . . . everybody knows in their bones that something is eternal, and that something has to do with human beings."

For centuries the chruch has affirmed, "I believe in the life everlasting." This belief is based on logic, intuition, faith, hope, and the assurances of the scriptures.

I shall discuss the personal element in immortality. I believe that personal relationships will continue on the highest level with God and others. While we cannot know the details of the life beyond, we think in terms of personality and recognition, growth and fulfillment. The Bible, too, seems to bear out this concept.

Grace Fletcher told about her father's experience in a New England parish. The doorbell rang one afternoon and one of his members, Molly Stark, stood without. She blurted as she greeted her pastor, "Lee, I have got to talk to you. I am going to die."

"We all are, Molly," the pastor replied. "Come in, and sit down and relax." Then she told the preacher about her malignancy, and her regret about leaving her ten-year-old son, Jimmy."

"You make it all seem so everyday," she said to Mr. Fletcher. "Funny, everybody has to die, but you never expect it to happen to you," she went on.

Then the pastor reminded Molly that what the people forget is that we are living in eternity right now. The Lord holds the past, the present, and the future together, safe in His hands.

The faith was also expressed that there would be renewed personal relationships.

We believe that the continuing life is real. The simple, direct narratives of the events of the resurrection bear every earmark of genuineness. Coming from the tomb a living personality, Christ convinced the disciples, including Thomas, who insisted on the identifying marks of the cross, that he was alive. "Last of all," Paul affirmed, "he appeared to me also."

With this conviction of the risen, living Lord, the whole climate of faith and religion changed in the early Christians. Broken and defeated men were thrilled with new life and power, and victory was wrought out of despair.

Countless Christians have since spoken of his living presence. Phillips Brooks once exclaimed, "God is the realest thing in the world to me. I know Him and He knows me."

When Josiah Royce, the noted philosopher, was asked to define a Christian, he looked out the window and saw the celebrated preacher. "There goes Phillips Brooks," he remarked. If, then, God is so real to a person here, will He not so continue in the hereafter?

The evangelist Dwight L. Moody also spoke of the reality of Christ's presence. Asked if he believed in the risen Lord, he replied, "Yes, indeed, I talked to him this morning."

To have eternal life is to embody spiritual values, and to be in right relationship with God. It is to keep the eternal light of Christ within and to radiate his love.

At times the light seems almost extinguished, but it is a living hope and assurance that never dies. It is a quality of spirit that will never perish, and of a life triumphant.

Speaking at a funeral service of a close friend, H. E. Fosdick said, "To be sure, the mystery of immortality is very great. It is not so much the survival of the spiritual life that is a mystery; it is the arrival of such a life in the first place. There is the mystery—the arrival of a quality of life, essentially timeless and eternal."

Things of lasting quality have a way of renewing themselves, and the hope eternal continues to beat in the human heart. Who has not felt that when the body of a loved one is laid aside, the fair and noble spirit was not consigned to the dust, but goes on living with the eternal God?

We believe, too, in the relevance of eternal life. Some assert they don't care about what lies beyond this life either for themselves or for others, but the vast majority of people accept its relevance and feel the need for such a hope.

The practical need for immortality was expressed by William James, "Because I am getting fit to live." On his seventy-fifth birthday Victor Hugo wrote, "Winter is on my head, but eternal spring is in my heart. I feel I have not said the thousandth part of what is in me. When I go down to the grave, I will say like others, I have finished my day's work, but I cannot say I have finished my life. . . . The tomb is not a blind alley; it is a thoroughfare. It closes with the twilight to open with the dawn."

So we do not think of life everlasting as a mere extension of time, which would be colorless and unbearable, though a weary maid declared, "I am going to do nothing forever and forever."

If we are to greet the unknown with a cheer, there must be the thought of continuing light and growth. Surely we can move into a new dimension, and the personality can mount to higher levels.

A father who lost a twelve-year-old son in an accident found consolation in the concept of continuous development: "It has come to me since that his life must be a life of growth." The tender life, he felt, would mature in the beyond.

So we have the assurance that the embarkation we call death means we are in a seaworthy craft, in the hands of God, moving to the eternal shores.

READ: John 17:1–5
PRAYER: Eternal God, we thank Thee for Christ, who came that we might have the abundant and everlasting life. Amen.

20   *LET US GIVE THANKS*
(*On Thanksgiving*)

An eleven-year-old boy, Jonah Adkins, wrote a letter on "What Thanksgiving Day Means to Me." "Dear Lord," he said in simple, childlike language, "I'm writing this letter to thank you for giving us a holiday like Thanksgiving Day. . . . Thank you for keeping us well and blessing our table. Thank you for our schools and stores and decorations around us.

"Thank you for Mom and Dad and for all the people around us. Thanksgiving Day shouldn't be only one day but every day in the year. . . . I can look around and see love and all the wonderful wildlife things . . . and for peace, we thank you, dear Lord."

The youth had an appreciation, not only for material things but for family, friends, and peace.

The spirit of thanksgiving includes a sense of values. A cynic was defined by Oscar Wilde as a "man who knows the price of everything, and the value of nothing." To learn the price of an article we have only to read figures, but to know the value of a thing is an achievement.

A man who made his living by recapping automobile tires,

Maurice Hirsch, studied art and painting in his spare time. Poking around in an auction store one day, he found a painting that was lost in the miscellaneous collection of dust-covered articles. Since the man knew something of the value of art, he possessed the painting at a nominal sum. Its worth was later estimated at thirty thousand dollars.

But there are spiritual values of friendship, love, freedom, that cannot be measured in terms of money.

The matchless beauty of the outward world, too, is a joy forever. Lilies peep up even in the marsh lands. Dandelions blossom in the dust and thrust up through the cracks of walls. Nature has splashed its colors in woods and fields, on hillsides and valley lands. All remind us this is our Father's world.

We are grateful for our heritage of freedom. On a New England tour in 1962, I walked the hallowed grounds at Plymouth, where our Founding Fathers settled in 1620. History came alive as I thought of the courage and sacrifice of the men and women who came over in crude sailing vessels across perilous unknown seas.

Sick with scurvy, influenza, and pneumonia, undernourished and weak, they were unable to cope with the infections of disease. They buried their children and laid away the mothers who went hungry to feed their children. Fathers perished in the unequal combat with weather, disease, and savages. When the spring finally came and the warm sun broke the grip of winter, half of the settlers were dead.

But in the autumn of 1621 their survivors had their Thanksgiving. The Indian Squanto had taught them how to plant maize, dropping a fish at each hill for fertilizer. "It was the Indian maize which built America, along with the ax and the stout heart," wrote Ralph McGill. So the Pilgrims gave thanks to God for their survival and the hope of a permanent settlement, mentioning corn in their prayers of gratitude.

Nor should we be ungrateful for those nearest of kin and for those with whom we are closely associated from day to day. We often take for granted those who do so much for our convenience and comfort in the home. The famous author Thomas Carlyle lived on a lonely farm near Dumfriesshire, Scotland. One evening at dinner his wife asked why he had never expressed appreciation for the many things she did for him.

Years later he read in the diary of his deceased wife, "Oh, I wish you had said a kind word or given me a compliment now and then about the things I tried to do to make you happy." Are we inclined to overlook some word of appreciation for loved ones?

The principal of an elementary school once suggested that the children write thank-you letters to the people in the community who had helped them in various ways. The idea caught fire and hundreds of letters were written to some who often receive no recognition or thanks. So spontaneous, warm words of appreciation went out to the postman, the milkman, the newspaper boy, the policeman, parents, teachers. The simple act of letter writing could brighten and bless many people.

A final thought concerning thanksgiving is the proper understanding of the word "blessing." A favor bestowed or a gift received is its usual connotation.

It was once felt that a good man was blessed and a bad man was blasted. The things that brought joy to a person were favors of God while pain and suffering were felt to be the frown of God.

But all sunshine and no storms have left many people soft, selfish, and spineless. Many who have come up the hard way of struggle and hardship have attained the goals of real character and achievement. By such experiences their insights have been deepened, understanding widened, sympathies heightened.

Paul spoke of his persecution or suffering as working out for the advancement of the gospel. See him in the Philippian jail or standing on the deck of a ship that was being pounded to pieces on an unknown coast, urging the people to "be of good cheer, for I believe God." Ever a grateful soul, Paul declared, "We know that in everything, God works for good with those who love him."

READ: Psalm 111

PRAYER: For all Thy blessings, both temporal and spiritual, we give Thee thanks, the Father of all mercies. For those experiences that enable us to grow and to develop all the potentialities with which Thou hast endowed us, we thank Thee. Amen.

21   AN ALL-HEALING LIGHT
(Christmas Season)

Some years ago a man took his little daughter to see the Statue of Liberty, in New York. She was unable to sleep that night and her father asked, "What is keeping you awake?" She replied: "Daddy, I am thinking of the lady with the lamp. She is standing out there all alone. Don't you think somebody ought to help her hold the lamp up?"

The hope of our world is for men of good will everywhere to lift high the torch of freedom. By doing so we may help to drive away the darkness of prejudice and hate, and bring peace on earth and good will among men.

When President John F. Kennedy was assassinated and other murders were committed during the tragic month of November, 1963, the darkness of resentment and hate came upon an unwary and complacent people.

Harking back to World War II, the conflict in which the lamented President nearly lost his life, many people have a haunting memory of blackouts. The reign of darkness was a symbol of the blackness of evil and bloodshed.

There is still an urgent need for us "to melt the cloud of sin and darkness." Consider that anything often goes under the curtain of darkness. Immorality and gambling are widespread. The cost of drinking soars into billions of dollars annually, far outweighing the amount spent on education or religion. There are deep shadows of misunderstanding, suspicions, and malice.

But the light of Christ still shines in the darkness. In his description of a 1952 bomb test in Nevada, David Lawrence wrote, "Then there was a light out of this world, with the intensity of a hundred suns." Our hope is not in nuclear bombs that could plunge the world into darkness, but in the greater intensity of the light and love of Christ.

Someone told of a little boy who was sent to bed on Christmas Eve. Fearing the darkness, he asked, "Can't I have a little light?" Then he looked out the window and saw a bright light, a star. "God has put a light in the sky for me!" he exclaimed. That is what God did for us in Christ, the Light of the world.

Candle-lighting at Christmastime was first introduced in America by Count Nicholas von Zinzendorf, leader of the Moravians. Lighting up a candle on Christmas Eve, 1741, he headed a procession to a stable in a small Pennsylvania town. Harking back to the birthday of our Lord, he said, "In memory of Christ, let this place be called Bethlehem."

Following the custom thus instituted, a large star is lighted every year on December 4 atop South Mountain, and a service is held in Zinzendorf Square.

The idea of illuminating other towns and cities spread rapidly. A hundred-foot star was lighted on Mill Mountain, Roanoke, Virginia, on Christmas Eve. Since then Roanoke has been called "the Star City" of the South.

Modern houses have a bright glow in windows against the bleakness of snow, cold, and rain during the Advent season. Home and community trees are illuminated, symbolic of the Light of the world. "Still the light shines in darkness, and the darkness has never put it out."

"You are the light of the world," Christ said. Men once walked the streets at twilight crying, "Hang out your light!" The householder was responsible for illuminating his surroundings.

We can let the light shine through the example of our lives.

As Gladstone observed, "One example is worth a thousand arguments." Principles must be practiced, creeds put into deeds.

A missionary returned from Japan some years ago and related her experience in a concentration camp during the war. Amid the darkness of her prison cell she kept repeating to herself, "All the darkness of the world cannot put out the light of a single candle." Refusing to return evil for evil, she let the light of love and forgiveness shine in her heart.

When Tokyo and its surrounding communities were nearly wiped out by earthquake and fire, one Christian leader held up the lamp of faith. Within a few hours the fruit of patient toil over decades seemed to be in ruins. But in the midst of the debris Bishop John McKim sent a message to the United States: "All gone but faith in God."

Inspired by the unshaken faith of one man, Christians in Japan and America joined hands in the task of rebuilding. Out of the ashes and the darkness around them, better schools, churches, and hospitals sprang up.

So, amid the difficulties and discouragements of life when the outlook seems very dark, the uplook to God may be bright and beckon us to a better future.

Above all, the light of love is at the heart of Christmas. Those who have the light within can change the dark picture that hangs over large areas of the world, and light the path for others.

A retired school teacher who had taught in one of the worst sections of Baltimore celebrated her eightieth birthday some time ago. Years before she had worked diligently, undiscouraged, with her seemingly unpromising students. She did more than dispense knowledge; she molded character and inspired the youth to make something of themselves.

As the years unfolded, they became doctors, lawyers, educators, preachers, skilled craftsmen, technicians. Now, on that anniversary occasion, the former students came to pay tribute to their much loved teacher.

When a reporter asked her about the secret that had made her work so successful, she replied, "Oh, I don't know. . . .

Young teachers in our school today are so well equipped with training and learning, I realized I was ill-prepared to teach. I had nothing to give them but love." That is what Christ gave to our world.

READ: Psalm 43:3–4; Matthew 5:14–16

PRAYER: In the midst of the darkness of our time, O God, send out Thy light. Help us to be bearers of the light. In Christ's name. Amen.

22 *WHEN THE WORD CAME ALIVE*
(*For Christmas Day*)

A little girl who received a portion of scripture with the Christmas story asked, "Does it tell about the angels, the star, and the baby?" When told that it did, she replied, "I'm going to say a little thank-you prayer when I read it." She had some appreciation of the spiritual significance of Christmas.

With commercial carols and Santa Claus at the center of Christmas, many children may wonder whose birthday we are observing. The occasion is also associated with exchanges of gifts, festivity, unbridled license, and dissipation.

But many are aware that we would suffer immeasurably if we lost the true meaning of Christmas. A brief address was made to a group of students by J. A. Dell on "I Dreamt That He Had Not Been Born." In his vision he dreamt that chaos was on the throne. The clock was turned back, and the whole structure of civilization tumbled in. Woman had a lowly position, and there were no schools. Freedom was blacked out. Life was emptied of any real significance. Suddenly the sleeper awakened. Then the relief! It was only a dream.

During the Advent season we re-affirm that Christ was born in our world, and lived among us in human form, "full of grace and truth."

Consider that the likeness of God comes to us in the Person of Christ. He becomes real and concrete to us in Jesus Christ. "Humanity seeks the ideal, but it seeks it in a Person," wrote Ernest Renan.

Someone told of a brilliant young man who was embittered because of the false claims of a religious cult. His mother had cancer, and she was told that she would be healed if she had enough faith. She died. "A lack of faith," some said! The son was naturally resentful.

He became an ardent Communist. He sought the counsel of a friend, and a reading of the gospel of Luke was recommended to him. The young Communist read Luke's gospel at one sitting, and was so fascinated, he exclaimed, "What a man!" Seeing Christ in a new light, as healer, friend of the needy, and outcast redeemer, he became a disciple of our Lord and an able preacher of the Word.

Taking on the flesh of man, Christ lived among the simple surroundings of the Galilean hills. "He became like as we are that he might make us as he is."

> He came down to earth from heaven
> Who is God and Lord of all,
> And his shelter was a stable,
> And his cradle was a stall.
> With the poor and mean and lowly
> Lived on earth our Savior holy.

> (*Royal David's "City Hymns for Little Children"*)

We use symbols and pictures to keep before us and make realistic the image of persons. In a city some years ago, my attention was called to the statues of notable men, a source of inspiration to thousands who paraded through the park.

Recall the famous statue of Christ in Copenhagen. A little boy who saw the disappointment written in the face of a spectator remarked, "Sir, you must come closer, kneel down at his feet and look into his face." By doing so the visitor saw the rare beauty and radiance on the face of Christ.

Pictures, too, make a silent impact on our lives, whether in the home or in public buildings. When a mother visited her son in college she noticed some pictures on the wall of the student's room that displeased her. She made no comment, but in a few days the boy received from her a well-known portrait of Christ. In a subsequent visit the parent observed that the obscene pictures had come down. "With the picture of Christ on the wall," said the student, "the others were out of place."

Consider also that the living Word or example speaks more eloquently than words from our lips. As Paul wrote: "You yourselves are our letter of recommendation . . . to be known and read of all men."

"A familiar example you see is always the most effective way to define a thing," said Liston Pope. The word "mother," for instance, is defined by *Webster's* as "female parent." When we think of the example of mother, it touches some of the deeper emotions of the heart.

A. J. Gossip dedicated a book to his parents in these words: "To the memory of Robert Gossip whose heart was as a little child's, and of Margaret Grieve Gossip in whose face I saw God's." Their images were stamped deeply on his mind and heart, for they were the living Word.

A well-known hymn writer, Isaac Watts, was characterized as "a bit of Christ."

While we may not rise to the spiritual level of Isaac Watts, we can show something of the likeness of Christ.

A pastor, Leslie Weatherhead, was called to a home where death had cast its shadow. A young wife was bitter, resentful, even hostile to God, because her husband had been slain in battle. As she languished in misery, an older woman's arm was around her shoulder, trying to console her in her distress.

"Where was God, to let this thing happen to my husband?" the young wife blurted.

Without trying to give a reasonable meaning of death, the

pastor told how the mother, through her sensitive and understanding spirit, was the comforting arm of God around her.
She was "a bit of Christ," in the time of greatest need. So in all
of life's experiences we may be the living example, showing
forth the spirit of our Lord.

As James E. Wagner said, "The heart and root of our
Christian faith is that God walked this earth and lived our life
in the Person of his Son Jesus Christ. . . . The Word became
flesh and dwelt among us."

READ: John 1:14–18; James, 1:22–27

PRAYER: We rejoice, O God, in the coming of Christ into
the world. Grant that we may know him as our Companion,
Guide, and Redeemer, and may become more and more like
him. Amen.

23   *THE BIBLE STILL SPEAKS*
(*On Bible Sunday*)

Ideas expressed in books have done more to change the ways
of man than guns and bombs. When the author of *Uncle Tom's
Cabin*, Harriet Beecher Stowe, was presented to Abraham Lincoln, he reportedly said, "So this is the little woman whose
book started a war." Other volumes, such as Hitler's *Mein
Kampf* and Karl Marx's *Das Kapital*, have shaken the founda-
tions of civilization.

The first book printed by the inventor of movable type was
the Bible. Finishing in 1456, Gutenberg spent six years in printing
the scriptures. The Gutenberg Bible weighed some twenty-eight
pounds. Besides being the oldest printed book, it is the most

attractive volume ever published. One copy sold for six hundred thousand dollars.

Today the Bible could be printed by electronics in seventy seconds, but to understand and appreciate the Word of God takes time. For many people it is crowded out by television programs, and the vast collection of books, magazines, and newspapers.

"Every month in America more than nine million pulp magazines are read," wrote Charles Crowe. Besides the exciting adventures of love, there are millions of confession publications. The total output, including comics, rockets to fifty-five million monthly.

Still the Bible inspires, enlightens, and redeems millions. Multitudes find faith, hope, and sustaining strength in its pages.

The scriptures are basic in our culture and civilization. Conversations are saturated with quotations or references to the Bible, such as "the signs of the times," "the second mile," "help from the hills."

Handel's *Messiah* sprang from the mind and heart of Isaiah's words on the suffering servant. The immortal paintings, Leonardo da Vinci's "Last Supper," Holman Hunt's "The Light of the World," and many others have grown out of the scriptures. Our moral and ethical structure have been lifted out of the Bible. World literature has flowed from its fountain.

We come face to face with God in the scriptures. His goodness and love are revealed. The concern and compassion of Christ are shown in the matchless stories of the good Samaritan and the prodigal son. The way of life is pointed out by our Lord: "I am the way, the truth, and the life."

In the Bible we learn that God loves all men and is concerned that His children live in good will and fellowship with one another. God is concerned with reclaiming and redeeming man from his sins.

False ideas of Christianity fall away with an understanding of the Bible. When General Wallace set out to write a book to expose the fallacies of the Christian religion, he made a thorough study of the Word in preparation for the assignment. By doing so Wallace was converted to Christ, and wrote a book on the beauty and divinity of Christ. His volume, entitled *Ben Hur*, won fame as best-seller and a movie production was based on it.

A new vision of man appears in the Bible. We are creatures of supreme worth and dignity in God's sight. But man is weak and sinful, and needs the compassion and forgiveness of God. Purity of motives, sincerity of life, humility and mercy, are emphasized in the New Testament. Spiritual values are to be lifted over material possessions, and we are to attain unto the fullness of life in Christ, not by our own merits but by the grace of God.

Uprightness and chastity are stressed in the scriptures as the essential virtues of man. Robert E. Goodrich, Jr., told of a young woman who went to a hotel room for an appointment of shame. Arriving early, she picked up a Gideon Bible and read a passage that gripped her mind and soul. Determined to turn away from her sordid past, she wrote a note about her experience and left the hotel. Becoming a new person in Christ, she heard the call to become a missionary.

We must bear a responsibility for our sins, for they effect not only the individual but others. One's conduct may even break the heart of another. A son returned home after he had spent three years in prison, still hard-hearted and unrepentant. His mother, once a beautiful woman, blooming and gay, had become worn, wrinkle-faced, stooped. As she opened the door to receive her wayward son, he burst into tears: "Oh, Mother, what have I done to you?" The sight of his mother stirred his heart as neither punishment nor prison had done.

Resources for living are available to those who let God speak to them through the Bible, and our lives are remolded by the discovery of the power of God. Uranium was once referred to as a metal that had no important uses. Now the splitting of the atom has made uranium a source of infinite power. So millions of people have found new resources of strength through prayer and devotional reading.

Field Marshal Montgomery was taught by his mother to read

the scriptures regularly and to memorize a verse every morning before breakfast. The habit stuck with him, and the Bible was his daily companion. It gave him an adequacy in life and work.

In time of emergency the Word of God can be our stay and strength. A couple went on an exploration trip in the vast area of Big Bend National Park. Soon after they had entered the park the car balked. The wife sought help, since her husband had a bad heart. In her mad search for aid she got lost in the wilderness and wandered around for six days. Weak from hunger and suffering from thirst, she told reporters later, "The Twenty-third Psalm kept running through my mind."

God was a very present help to her as she kept repeating: "The Lord is my shepherd, I shall not want. . . ." She found comfort, too, to help her in the loss of her husband, who failed to survive the ordeal in the park.

READ: I Samuel 9:27; Psalm 119:105

PRAYER: Make Thy Word "a lamp to our feet, a light to our path," O Lord, that we may not stumble in darkness, but walk in the light of Thy wisdom and truth. In Christ's name. Amen.

24 *SURVIVAL IS NOT ENOUGH*
(*World Peace*)

What is the number one problem of our space age? Is it outracing Russia to the moon or to one of the planets? Is it the problem of population explosion or unemployment? Is it the race issue?

The quest of the ages seems to focus on one thing—human relations. Recall the memorable, oft-quoted words of Franklin D. Roosevelt: "We are faced with the pre-eminent fact that if civilization is to survive we must cultivate the science of human relationships—the ability of all kinds of people to live together and work together in the same world at peace."

We cannot be unmindful of our interrelatedness today. The movie *The Defiant Ones* tells of two prisoners who escaped from a chain gang. The white prisoner, John Jackson, and the Negro prisoner, Noah Cullen, are bound together and are bitter with each other. Dashing away into the wilderness, they fuss and fume. One falls into the ditch, and the other must help him or stay by the horrible pit. The picture symbolizes the predicament of the human race.

While many would like to escape from involvement in the human situation, and leave some in the ditch of misery and misunderstanding, the day of judgment eventually comes.

In a facetious vein, the desire to run away from responsibility may be pointed up by the story of a preacher who was walking home one night and fell into a hole. A church member came that way to investigate. Soon he discovered the minister's dilemma, but did nothing immediately to lift him out of the pit. Instead, the man said, "Well, you need not be kicking up such a rumpus, for this is only Wednesday night, and we won't be needing you before Sunday."

If we are to have peace in our world we must do more than take the defensive measures of building air shelters and heaping up armaments. In the race for peace the essential elements are mutual understanding, cooperation, and recognition of the basic needs of all mankind.

We must make democracy work effectively in our country, and thus prove the superiority of our way of life. Consider some of the dark spots in our society. Alcohol and narcotics are a widespread indulgence, symptomatic of maladjustments and unhappiness in millions. Dishonesty in high and low places has shocked the nation. Race conflicts and mob violence have had global repercussions.

War madness has been a setback to civilization. In the past four thousand years there have been less than three hundred years of peace. The book *A Study of War*, by Quincy Wright, gives statistics showing there were 492 wars in 461 years. Major conflicts in the first half of the twentieth century have caused a colossal waste of property and human life.

A nuclear war would be far worse than any past conflict. The *Polaris* submarine, for example, is called a "city killer." Sixteen missiles are carried on the *Polaris* and each one is twenty-five times as powerful as the bomb that destroyed Hiroshima.

In the task of peacemaking we should be mindful that nations are made up of individuals created in our own likeness, with common needs of "bread, beauty, and brotherhood." We are fellow human beings with similar desires, heartaches, and aspirations.

A prize story, "The Man I Didn't Kill," by André Chamson, was published in *Reader's Digest* of October, 1962. On a bitter cold day Chamson was on a mission of reconnaissance. Nearing the enemy lookout line, at the bottom of a ravine, he saw a German sentinel. Lifting his gun, Chamson aimed carefully at the soldier whose back was turned to him. But just as he was about to fire, the German began to jump about and to swing his arms. Then he realized what had seemed a target a moment ago was a fellow human being, suffering from the cold.

"The piercing cold, suffered in common, had made us brothers," he wrote. "Who among us could kill his fellow man if he actually knew him? . . . If each of us could be personally known to his fellow man . . . there would never be another war." So if we had an understanding relationship and appreciation for others, we would live forever in peace.

There are three R's that we should remember.

(1) The recognition that we are bound together in a human chain. A painting in England shows how a soldier was sent to the front line in battle to inspect communication cables. The messages conveyed through these lines saved many lives.

But the communication system was disrupted when one of the wires snapped. Nor did the soldier have repair tools with him. So, with enemy shells bursting around him, he caught one end of the wire in his left hand and stretching his right hand, he gripped the other end. In such manner he became a vital part of the communication system. Individuals make up a country, and each one bears some influence upon another. We are a link in the chain of world fellowship.

(2) The reconciliation of persons, races, and nations must be effected to establish the ways of brotherhood and world peace. The little things and un-Christian attitudes often cause conflict and drive people apart.

Two men fell out over a line fence and did not speak to each other for a long time, the story goes. But one of the men was very unhappy about the estranged relationship. Taking the Bible one day to his neighbor, he said, "John, you read and I will pray." Then he handed the Bible to his neighbor and added, "We must be friends."

"I can't read," John, the neighbor, mumbled. "I haven't my glasses." "Take mine," Jim, the peacemaker, urged. After the Word of God was read and Jim prayed, the men embraced each other. Giving the Bible back to his neighbor, John spoke through tears of joy, "Jim, that old fence looks different through your glasses." People everywhere look different if we see them through the eyes of Christ, and broken relationships are mended by showing his spirit.

(3) Religion is the basis of right relations with people of the earth. The noted historian Arnold Toynbee wrote: "The West has erred because it has chosen to fight Communism with their own material weapons. The West must base its appeal in more than prosperity; it must appeal to religion. . . . The grace of God must bring about the miracle."

Peacemaking, whether among ourselves or nations, hinges on our cooperation with God, the divine and spiritual encounter. It denotes the breaking down of the barriers of misunderstanding, bitterness, rebellion against God and man. It means widening the areas of community and world fellowship.

While the vast spending of our resources at home together with our give-away program overseas has helped people and nations, it has tended to dim the sights of men on the moral basis of our society. Money is not the messiah that some have claimed in either the Communist or the free world.

We need today a new commitment of our lives to the lordship of Christ, and to moral and spiritual principles. We need a new sense of involvement in establishing right human relations, even beyond our own personal and immediate concerns.

The story comes from India of a man who was in a small boat when a severe storm rocked it so violently that he was in jeopardy of his life. In a time of crisis he promised his god everything, even his yoke of oxen. When the tempest quieted down, however, and he reached the land, he gave his lord only a few nuts and shells, the leftovers.

Our religion must again match the fiery spirit of the early Christians who "outlived and outloved" others, and who helped to turn the world right-side up.

Our real strength is to be found in the intellectual, moral, and spiritual dimension. To win in the tremendous struggle with secularism and Communism we must use what Charles Malik called "the total arsenal of political, moral, and spiritual values."

READ: Hebrews 11:32, 12:12–16

PRAYER: May we know, Eternal God, "we cannot survive materially unless we are redeemed spiritually." In Christ's name. Amen.